UNCURATED
SOUND

UNCURATING SOUND

Knowledge with Voice and Hands

Salomé Voegelin

BLOOMSBURY ACADEMIC
NEW YORK • LONDON • OXFORD • NEW DELHI • SYDNEY

BLOOMSBURY ACADEMIC
Bloomsbury Publishing Inc
1385 Broadway, New York, NY 10018, USA
50 Bedford Square, London, WC1B 3DP, UK
29 Earlsfort Terrace, Dublin 2, Ireland

BLOOMSBURY, BLOOMSBURY ACADEMIC and the Diana logo are trademarks of
Bloomsbury Publishing Plc

First published in the United States of America 2023

Library of Congress Cataloging-in-Publication Data
Names: Voegelin, Salomé, author.
Title: Uncurating sound : knowledge with voice and hands / Salomé Voegelin.
Description: New York : Bloomsbury Academic, 2023. |
Includes bibliographical references and index. | Summary: "A discussion of the
topics of curation, geography, and material production in the context of
sound studies and the sonic world"– Provided by publisher.
Identifiers: LCCN 2022031331 (print) | LCCN 2022031332 (ebook) |
ISBN 9781501345418 (hardback) | ISBN 9781501345401 (paperback) |
ISBN 9781501345425 (epub) | ISBN 9781501345432 (pdf) |
ISBN 9781501345449 (ebook other)
Subjects: LCSH: Sounds–Philosophy. | Sounds–Social aspects. | Curatorship.
Classification: LCC B105.S59 V66 2023 (print) | LCC B105.S59 (ebook) |
DDC 110–dc23/eng/20220826
LC record available at https://lccn.loc.gov/2022031331
LC ebook record available at https://lccn.loc.gov/2022031332

ISBN: HB: 978-1-5013-4541-8
PB: 978-1-5013-4540-1
ePDF: 978-1-5013-4543-2
eBook: 978-1-5013-4542-5

Typeset by Newgen KnowledgeWorks Pvt. Ltd., Chennai, India
Printed and bound in Great Britain

To find out more about our authors and books visit www.bloomsbury.com
and sign up for our newsletters.

CONTENTS

ACKNOWLEDGEMENTS

The pandemic made it very apparent that writing is a conversation and needs a conversation to sustain itself against the muteness of isolation, to be able to write the condition of our *being with*, with each other and with more than human bodies and things. I am grateful therefore to everybody who, despite the need for distance, I was in contact with. Every voice I heard helped my thoughts and ideas to develop, to write against the lockdown and social distancing a book that hopes to continue and expand these conversations and generate a critical proximity from shared words.

This book was written in a changing time that stretches conventions and how we live together. I want to thank my family for providing continuity and a sense of place in a time of upheaval and change. And I want to particularly thank David Mollin for his unfaltering critical engagement in my work and writing and our long-standing collaboration. I want to thank Mark Peter Wright, Anna Barney, Phoebe Stubbs and Timothy Smith, for critical discussions and co-working in the context of Listening across Disciplines II, which kept my thoughts moving on the transversality of sound. I am immensely grateful to Evgeny Bylina (HSE Art and Design School, editor of a book series The History of Sound at The New Literary Observer), whose invitations to write and speak helped prepare three of the chapters. I am also grateful to Christophe Fellay, for the opportunity to perform as part of 'être à l'écoute' a symposium on sound at L'EDHEA (école de design et haute école d'art du Valais) Sierre, Switzerland, which informed the performance score printed in this book. I want to say a special thanks to Peter Kiefer with whom it was a pleasure to develop a close professional relationship against the distance demanded by the pandemic, and also to Holger Schulze, Ania Mauruschat, Kate Donovan, Heather Frasch, Peter Cusack, Brandon LaBelle, Michael Fowler and others who, since my arrival in Berlin, have been regular walk and talk companions to make sense of the world through sounding and listening. I am grateful to Åsa Stjerna for a great year at HBK Braunschweig together and to Zey Suka-Bill for her support of my hiatus, which was invaluable to make me think a different way. I am appreciative of the research environment of CRiSAP (Centre for Research in Sound Arts Practice) at the London College of Communication (LCC), UAL, Cathy Lane, Lisa Hall, Thomas Gardner, Angus Carlyle and Rob Mullender, whose research and work inspires my own. I have profited immensely from co-working and co-thinking with Kate Carr of Flaming Pines and have valued critical discussions on race, class, education and sound with Kevin Logan, Kerstin Meissner and Nicole Brittingham Furlonge. I am grateful for the many invitations to speak and be in conversation, online and in real life, that have enabled connectivity and exchange. And so I thank Cécile Malaspina, Ramona Mosse, Thibault Walter, Sabine Sanio, Søren Kjærgaard, Luís Cláudio Ribeir and many more. Finally, I want to thank Leah Babb-Rosenfeld at Bloomsbury for her trust and support when writing was difficult.

PROLOGUE

Sounding Gaps in Pavements

Walk along a pavement
Made from paving slabs
Taking care never to stand on a gap
Every time you do, make a sound.

Walking on pavements while avoiding standing on the gaps between paving slabs is a game. It is a playful participation in the design of the civic infrastructure. But it is also an attempt to find a rhythm and a voice within or against that very infrastructure. To resist its lines by moving against their design: performing the body and what it touches, what rhythms it makes, and performing the environment, what shape it takes by how I move within it. While larger paving slabs invite this game, cobblestoned roads do not permit me this performance easily. The gaps are too many, too irregular, too close together, the surface too uneven and slippery. If I try to avoid the in-between and want to make a neat pattern, I have to dance in tiny steps; my feet will lose their rhythm and I will fall over. Tarmacked pavements on the other hand give me no such engagement, as their smooth surface pretends that there are no gaps, no in-between, that everything is the same, a flat continuum. Until I hit a road. And so I rather dance on cobblestones, not really getting anywhere, falling over, falling into gaps and enjoying the disorder and variability of uneven surfaces and a slippery ground.

Scholarly writing has an infrastructure and an institutional design that draws lines and sets a tone, which as register organizes and validates knowledge, its presentation and form. It does so through evidence and interpretation, and relies on critical language to make thought legible and recognizable, and thus accessible, as well as to give it validity through reference and context. This intelligibility, from which meaning is derived, and which in turn gives it value, however, depends on a certain understanding of format and voice: what a text can talk about and how it can speak. To write beside the lines, to evoke a different register, and eschew evidence in favour of narration and contingent experience, creates disorder. Since, to abandon the line is to lose history and geography as spectres of criticality and definition, to become ill-defined and problematic.

But when the talking with cannot preclude understanding in a homogeneous group, then communication cannot soundlessly refer to principles, to canonical texts and a universal truth, but becomes about revealing and sharing what cannot be assumed, what cannot be shared. Such writing is about performing difference and questioning the idea of validity in reference, as an understood and agreed-upon idea, in favour of contingent and contextual speculations: to narrate and imagine rather than evidence.

Writing the institution depends on a cultural agreement on what constitutes a scholarly text, a legitimate argument, a recognizable method, content, and so on. These conventions are strongest when they are not spoken but adhered to quietly in the mechanism of (anonymous) review and validation; where the burden of evidence falls on muted writing, to show a historical and linear reference and imagination, which might seem true but which excludes, into the future, what does not follow backwards on that line. Such evidence does not come from practice or conversation, which is imbued with possibility and lived narration. Instead, it comes from a sense of actuality and validity, derived from what has been said already. It talks always and by necessity with a historical voice, determining the scope of the self and by extension of the other, in reference to a time-geographical frame and register where what we know makes possible what else can be known, as everything else remains impossible, and where the notion of critique becomes an effort of exclusion, of keeping out what speaks in another register and with a different voice, rather than caring for words not yet said and producing an inclusive network of knowledge and sense.

But what about the voice that cannot find itself in that historico-geographical space? What about the self and other whose voice does not write to continue that line, or whose lines are unrecognizable, fragmented, diffuse, invisible?

'What is my place
if I am a woman? I look for myself throughout the centuries and don't see myself anywhere' … 'Where to stand? Who to be?'[1]

---

[1]Hélène Cixous and Catherine Clément, *The Newly Born Woman* (London: I. B. Tauris, 1996), 75.

For the word 'woman' in Hélène Cixous and Catherine Clément's text the *Newly Born Woman* from 1975, we can insert our own exclusions, manifold and off-centre places from which we write.

'What is my place
if I am … ?'
           … 'Where to stand? Who to be?'

How to write?

To think of another writing that has your ear in my voice and lets your hands extend its sound.

Since, whoever I am, I am caught, always already, in the form of the text and the conventions of language, which as a frame organizes the very order that makes what I hope to say invisible.

How do I write then, a 'disorganized' voice and a 'disorganized' text?

A book that is not evidenced through history and reference but writes in conversation a contingent narrative that materializes sense rather than interprets its meaning.

To put it another way, we have a deep curiosity about whether the language of the material and materialization might have different epistemological and political effects from the language of interpretation and the subject. … How might we talk strongly about 'the material' post the necessary intervention of discourse, and why does it matter?[2]

How do I write beside the line? In order not to strengthen, again and again, a singular and linear history but to open an expansive field of plural providence and inexhaustible futures.

How do I unform a book, its writing, its structure; the frame of reference and the voice of legitimacy, and still write a book?

Such a book provides no one message. No clear conclusion can be drawn. Instead, it performs its own presence that generates a disorder of connections and does not say what things mean but makes them mean by materializing them through words beside and with each other as plural voices in incongruence but never in contradiction. The meaning then is found in participation, and the value of this interaction, if there is

---

[2]Alison Jones and Kuni Jenkins, 'Indigenous Discourse and "the Material", A Post-Interpretivist Argument', *International Review of Qualitative Research* 1, no. 2 (August 2008): 125–44, 127.

any, exists in my desire to collaborate: to find my voice in reading yours aloud. This might feel haphazard and tautological. And it might appear formless and senseless, like the sounds I emit when sliding on the uneven surface and slippery ground of the pebble-stoned road. But it is where instruction ends and conversation starts as a reciprocal event: where meaning is not gleaned from 'this' or 'that' but from the in-between, from the space between our bodies dancing on an unsteady path, and where accessibility does not signify comprehension, as a grasping of matter and things, but means as *being with* and through participation, and invites to sing your own voice.

Singing to claim what was considered private and public in the past and subvert it.[3]

The rigour of such writing cannot be deferred onto the past or onto an over-there, but has to be found on the body. The body thinking, writing, reading out loud, performing words as a muscular engagement with the world, whose actuality in turn is felt on the body, as fleshly and material form: as human and more than human matter that comes to matter from their in-between and in conversation. Thus, truth is not found as evidence, but as present memory, that witnesses from plural orientations the sense of contingent interactions. Therefore, I write a text that does not produce a theoretical voice, that I cannot lean on, that is not done, that does not have one form, but that I need to perform, again and again as a refrain that does not repeat but produces ever new layers through which we pass in the process of reading, as writing, as materialization.

And so, I learn to write and read another text that does not deliver but makes me do, always now, and that does not order to find out what is already here but performs a contingent order of other possibilities, whose rigour and orientation is plural and mobile.

We are not interested, in other words, in simply producing yet another feminist reflection on the body, nor yet in privileging the personal voice as a response to the 'victim' status so often assumed in the past. The deployment of the autobiographical voice is a deliberate strategy, … but what it speaks to is not nostalgia for the subject fully present to

---

[3]Aleyda Rocha Sepulveda, 'Territorialising from Within: protocolos [en tránsito] para atender lo de adentro', *Border-Listening/Escucha-Liminal* 1 (2020): 102.

herself, but rather the possibility of mobilising a series of differentially embodied and multiple I-slots.[4]

This, then, is a writing that sings to practice the plural simultaneity of words without a lexical definition or a grammatical line. Instead, it invites us into a dark motility to dance not on the surface of language but within 'unconventional dimensions', which we inhabit in sounding and listening and through which we can deviate from historical traditions and transform language's view, not by proposing another, not by erasure, but by seeing everything at once.

> I can! I can see all the stars everywhere. And I can see Ve Port and I can
> see anything
> I want! … And there is a planet, there is too! No don't hold me! Don't!
> Let me go![5]

The question is then not where does the margin begin, but what is it made of and where does it end. What can it touch and what is it touched by, without going via a central position but from all directions and into the future – block-chain like, mobile, and abundant, everywhere.

'The process of becoming material surfaces tensions, prompting us to inquire: *Who defines the material of the body? Who gives it value – and why?*'[6] (emphasis in original).

Stand in front of a mirror and repeat 'why am I, I?' one hundred times.

The 'I' of writing in conventional language forgets to ask this question and does not indulge in the dizzy disorientation of its repetitive chant. Instead, it hides any lingering doubt about its own position in the third person. Here it is not mobilized but fixed in an authoritative role that affixes the pretence of a neutral truth and a universalizing knowledge. He writes as he, whose 'I' is reflected in the tone and register of the institution, but without a body, and while this enables his text, it limits experience to the line of writing.

Whose 'I' matters?

---

[4]Margrit Shildrick and Janet Price, *Vital Signs, Feminists Reconfigurations of the Bio/logical Body* (Edinburgh, UK: Edinburgh University Press, 1998), 9.
[5]Ursula K. Le Guin, *The Unreal and the Real Volume 2: Selected Stories: Outer Space, Inner Lands* (London: Orion, 2015), 86.
[6]Legacy Russell, *Glitch Feminism, A Manifesto* (London: Verso, 2020), 9.

We are called the same 'I' but so very different.

Susan McClary received death threats for looking for a social meaning in music,[7] Luce Irigaray was dismissed from her teaching position for writing *Speculum of the Other Woman*,[8] Simone de Beauvoir's academic achievements were overshadowed by an interest in her personal life[9] and Audre Lorde was conscious of the total dismissal of her knowledge as a Black lesbian,[10] …

and all the invisible, unuttered discriminations, exclusions, dismissals and threats, loud and inaudible, that hassle and stain the writing and thinking of the other, … those who do not fit within an ordered view.

Whose order counts?

Research, scholarly writing and its review are not necessarily benign. It is not always generated from a generosity and curiosity of how else things could be, how things could be thought, could be written, could be read, beyond the line, in the disorder of what we do not yet know and do not know how to organize, as in grasp and instrumentalize to our own ends. Instead, it is a chauvinist battleground that defends a language made from power and control, built on fear of proximity and the anxiety of an unreliable body as well as from a sense of entitlement and self-evidence based on the paternal line.

Who sets the lines of power that make me dance with tiny steps, to trip up and fall?

It is not true that the shortest path between two points is the
      Straight line!

---

[7]Susan McClary and Sam de Boise, 'An Interview with Professor Susan McClary: The Development of Research on Gender and Music', *Per Musi: Scholarly Music Journal* 39 (2019): 1–9, e193906.

[8]*Speculum de l'autre femme* (1974; *Speculum of the Other Woman*), which was highly critical of Freudian and Lacanian psychoanalysis, resulted in her dismissal from her teaching position at Vincennes and the École Freudienne.

[9]'A scholar lecturing with de Beauvoir chastised their "distinguished [Harvard] audience [because] every question asked about Sartre concerned his work, while all those asked about Beauvoir concerned her personal life."' *Smart Encyclopedia*, July 2019, https://smartencyclopedia.org/content/simone-de-beauvoir/.

[10]Audre Lorde, 'The Master's Tools Will Never Dismantle the Master's House', *Your Silence Will Not Protect You* (Madrid, Spain: Silver Press, 2017), 90.

That is what I learnt when I was with you!
Dialogue? Is the longest part between the heart and the lips,
between my voiced waves and your silent waves.[11]

Because, rather than entering into conversation with the body as it sings, conventional language, as organizing text, seeks to capture material explosions in the muteness of theoretical writing: to 'domesticate' the voice of the other into the order of the familiar and to colonize speech; to find rationality and sense by avoiding the simultaneous dimensionality opened in its breath.

Coloniality is an investment in a singular and mute order. Its need for domination expresses the anxiety of the other, the fear of proximity and of contagion, of an untidy, ungraspable world and the paradox of a burning need to grasp it. To this imperative, grammar steadies unreliable speech, reference removes the mobile body, evidence clarifies the depth of the voice.

In turn, this order is the violence of the text, and of language, that organizes the form and colour of the line and of bodies, speaking and spoken to.

Decolonization, which sets out to change the order of the world, is, obviously, a program of complete disorder. But it cannot come as a result of magical practices, nor of a natural shock, nor of a friendly understanding.[12]

How can it come?

Decolonization, as we know, is a historical process: that is to say that it cannot be understood, it cannot become intelligible nor clear to itself except in the exact measure that we can discern the movements which give it historical form and content.[13]

---

[11]Ghada Al-Samman, 'The Lover of Blue Writing above the Sea!' (excerpt), in *The Poetry of Arab Women, A Contemporary Anthology*, trans. Saad Ahmed and Miriam Cooke, ed. Nathalie Handal (Northampton, MA: Interlink Books, 2015), 274–6.

[12]Franz Fanon, *The Wretched of the Earth*, 1961, quoted in Bonaventure Soh Bejeng Ndikung, 'Where Do We Go from Here: For They Shall Be Heard', *Frieze*, online, 28 October 2018, https://www.frieze.com/article/where-do-we-go-here-they-shall-be-heard (accessed August 2021).

[13]Franz Fanon, *The Wretched of the Earth*, trans. Constance Farrington (New York: Grove Press, 1961), 35.

These are movements we perform in judgement and validation, in peer review and examination or any other name we give to the process of selection and critique. Are we careful and caring? Are we willing to step into the disorder of another voice and feel our way through the text, not to reach the message we are looking for, but lingering in impressions, ideas and the jouissance of participation to find another way to sense? Or do we instinctively take on the baton of order and organization, taking on a righteous voice that knows the field and keeps it clean?

The mark-up becomes the gap in the paving stone which sets the rhythm of giving instructions and lets us trip up. It makes a line, and presents the desire to make the text fall in line.

I often hear a patriarchal voice performing my own mark-ups and critical commentary – voicing the demand to bring things in line, to communicate a message, to present clarity of thought and a line of evidence that legitimates, when all I want is to trouble lines and make connections that blur them even further, and write in the space beside and between, to generate a sensory sense rather than its interpretation.

I wanted to start by saying something about critique. I am not interested in critique. In my opinion, critique is over-rated, over-emphasized, and over-utilized, to the detriment of feminism.[14]

How to legitimate that?

How to have an enabling institution and keep it formless and disordered to hold the potential of a plural voice and to build a cobbled infrastructure, one that does not look for standardization, but an open practice from the in-between: performing an undisciplined dance of entanglements and diffuse connections?

To succeed in building such an open institution and keep its disorder, we might need regular reminders and useful scores to practice lingering and dancing, to keep the urge for control and the violence of the line at bay.

Draw a line
Redraw it
Use the breach to unsee the line

---

[14]Karen Barad, interviewed in Rick Dolphijn and Iris van der Tuin, *New Materialism: Interviews & Cartographies* (Ann Arbor, MI: Open Humanities Press, 2012), 49.

Can we ever overcome the orders and patterns that have been passed on to us and that we have re-created ourselves for our lives, to function, to fit in, following the sound of what we are called rather than calling ourselves?

To be, as Becket's Not I, at once not I and I, an idiosyncratic subjectivity that carries its plural name in its mouth.[15]

Because, if we would divest ourselves of theory's structure and deviate from its aim of legitimacy which is confirmed through reference, historico-geographical evidence and a mute voice, we could find meaning and intelligibility in plural voices, that materialize, that sing and hum and listen, simultaneously. To hear an order that remains unordered and undisciplined; that is contingent and provisional, a negotiation of resources, asymmetries, (mis)understandings, coincidences, bodies, materials and things and that finds legitimacy in performance.

In this sense, the game of standing or not on the gaps between paving slabs is a play of (dis)order and resistance. The uncoordinated and awkward steps made to stand clear of the line, and the playful urge for the deliberate foot down on the gap, or the petulant, and even wilful jump on exactly this spot where the earth shines through and small grass might grow, defy the need for order. Thus, from the play with this gap, we can start to defy the need for an orderly view and can enjoy where slabs move and collide. And I can dance on cobblestones, falling over, falling into gaps and enjoying the disorder and variability as an opening for other possibilities.

From that moment of whimsical anarchy, we can bring down the visual infrastructure of politics and of art: singing and dancing on an unsteady ground, we trouble its homogeneous surface, opening the gaps that language and reference filled, and wonder why we kept it intact for so long.

Fill your lungs with as much air as you can.
Sing without words until you are out of breath.

---

[15]Salomé Voegelin, 'Singing Philosophy: Deviating Voices and Rhythms without a Time Signature', *Open Philosophy* 4 (2021): 284–91, 289.

Introduction

Taking a breath together

was meant or had hoped, and set for my own deadline, to write this book more than two years ago. I had set this goal before the COVID pandemic started in 2019. The aim was to finish it by mid-2020. Two years after the last, a good rhythm for a little book. A little reprise, a syncopated thought on the three that had preceded it at regular four-year intervals. To make a slightly different move and take a critical stance at a discourse on sound that had grown exponentially into a diverse and complex, idiosyncratic, emerging and also still ignored discourse and way of seeing the world.

But I could not write it, and pushed the deadline three times. In hindsight, I believe this was because the isolation of COVID meant I could not listen and participate beyond myself. I could not hear people and speak and be in discussion in a space together during the pandemic. And so, I could not write, since writing is an act of responding, of being in conversation with, and once that conversation had moved online, the lack of an actual *being with*, of hearing each other and hearing my other in your voice, resonating through our shared space, seemed to stop my ability to write beyond my locked down and isolated body.

Initially, the isolation was scary, but novel enough to find some resource and get through it, to generate a different rhythm and another aim. We were very lucky living where we did with the woods nearby. A small living space compensated for by woods, a shared garden and the opportunity to use an absent neighbour's flat for work. Dangling an ethernet cable out of our window to reach theirs, like an umbilical cord and a precarious thread to the digitally connected world online. Throughout lockdown that cable kept me with people, albeit without the reverberations of a shared space. And so I enjoyed online connections, but I also never came to know what I might have started to hear had it snapped.

Ensconced in this way, the sonic world became smaller. Focused on my own body, my breathing, my movements, my sounding with walls and windows and other more than human bodies increasingly took on a more central role.

Breathing
Breathe normally
Listen to your breath
in and out, in and out, in and out …
stop breathing.

With only my family as an unwitting and unavoidable audience and participant in any sound making and listening, the voice turned inwards to its own materiality and source and found the body in the process of writing and thinking. And thus, while this moment did not lend itself to write something new, to find a different voice, it presented an ideal environment to write a revised second edition of *Sonic Possible Worlds: Hearing the Continuum of Sound*, published in 2014, to reflect back on its proposition of a world made from invisible and plural possibilities and to add a new chapter on the sonic possible and impossible body that I was now so intimately and exclusively in conversation with. The pandemic created the condition to think on the possibility of the body through and on my own locked down/isolated body. Its demands to quarantine created an intense focus on myself, while the threat of contagion highlighted this 'myself' not as an individuated being but as a porous, permeable extended body that was with every other body in sound and in the viral condition, which both reveal the delusions of the singular, the separate, and heighten an awareness of our codependence and the extent to which we always already *inter-are*.

Covid made this inter-being codependency apparent while sound makes it thinkable. The viral contagion evidences how the body does not end at the skin but expands like its sound and breath beyond, into a sphere to which we all belong, and in which we are as skinless, formless, unprotected flesh open to contagion. Thus, the pandemic recomposed the sense of self and sovereignty through a codependent reciprocity that as vulnerability demands responsibility. Our viral impact on each other emphasizes the impossibility of distance, as measure of safety and objectivity, and instead foregrounds the criticality of closeness as care. Therefore, instead of writing this book I knocked on walls, I licked windows, I performed and scored the house and interacted with more than human bodies as a means to practice distance against itself. To push against it and with it, to test and feel the possibilities and impossibilities of my body not through a singular reflection and a skin-made boundary wall, but through how it is made porous and in the proximity with other material and flesh bodies.

Lick Score
Stand in front of a window
Preferably one overlooking a busy street
Start cleaning the window with your tongue
Making loud sloshing sounds.

After licking windows, knocking on walls, walking in woods and leaning into the digital on a precarious ethernet line suspended outside. And after moving to another country, and finally hearing people again sharing a room and being in conversation, I now really aim to write this small volume in the form of chapters and performance scores. These are texts and textual rhythms that try to uncurate sound and uncurate knowledge with ears and hands and an idiosyncratic voice; to ponder the normal through the notion of a postnormality, as a different aspiration. Not to go back but to go forward into another possibility. To imagine how things could be after the experience of the pandemic, understood as the consequence of the celebration of toxic normativity. How we could care for each other and how we could understand where knowledge connects on open skins, to make a plural field of the local, the feminist, the decolonial and the tacit, and to reveal the universalizing violence of science and art.

However, now I do not just want to write a reprise. I no longer want to do a retake nor make a little syncopated move along a line that however troubled or off beat remains a continuation. Instead, I hope to announce that the line is lost, finally, in the diffusion of the viral load. That now reality and its evidence are a fuzzy geography of connected and plural knowledges and of people and things that trouble lines and live in the disruption as their own home made from sound. Because the pandemic revealed bodies in their plural and temporal forms and generated a sonic cosmopolitanism of breath and air, through which we can think climate and pollution, pandemics and politics, people and economics, and how we have divided up the indivisible to reap the consequences of this division's asymmetries.

I can write this now, even if late, and because it is late, in the sense of after and post-normativity. I can write this now because I re-found the other in myself through your voice. It is by sitting now again with people in proximity, hearing them perform ideas and desires, critiques and dreams, in a reverberant space, and inviting me to perform mine, that words can be written that do not theorize but generate. I write first with a pencil on a notepad as they speak, and then by sounding those words aloud and in response. I write ideas through my body from notes on your voice, which I get into conversations with, expand and return, to reciprocate a body in porous plurality.[1]

As I write this, I am sitting on a train with a PPF2 mask firmly on my face. And so I know the pandemic is not over, and I do not dare to pre-empt its end. In any event, I do not see it as an end but as ushering in a new era where pandemics remain and will come back, regularly, caused by humans ignoring the world's invisible dimension and codependency: its relational and connecting logic, from which we could conjure a way of thinking and living, with human and more than human bodies, in care and responsibility. And from where we could focus on the in-between and *being with*, to abandon the visual certainties and values that exploit the world's resources and each other for the delusions of an individuated body, with a separate fate and individual success that cannot see the antimony of its desire: to succeed alone is not to succeed at all, because in a sonic cosmos, binaries haunt each other in the same breath.

The following five chapters, one a performance score, and two shorter text-scores, write a conversation and try accessibility and intelligibility not through reference to lines and in evidence of things already said, but through the rhythm of breathing together, with other texts, and works and with the reader. Thus, the chapters and scores continue each other in multiple directions. There is no need to read them in order, one after the other. Their dialogue leans backwards and forwards, out of line, and responds across texts and ideas transversally from art into literature and into politics, and turning back always to the possibilities of the everyday.

The first discusses 'Curating politics in the gallery space'. It focuses on care in the word curation and reveals the violence of art and its organization. From there it tends to the notion of 'uncurating', which titles the book as a whole and identifies its aim as a deliberation between art, politics, knowledge and normativity. Whereby uncurating is not a rejection of curation, but is a reconsideration of the curatorial as an aesthetic, material and political as well as a knowledge project, whose history and ideology stretch along straight lines to confer legitimacy and reliability but omit care and plurality, which move on less visible paths. From there, and considering

---

[1]The initial notes for this introduction were written, in a hopeful mood, as scribbles on the program sheet of one of the first events I attended in real space and time, at SAVVY Contemporary in Berlin, in October 2021, *Here History Began*.

Kara Walker's work, this chapter invites the reperformance of the curatorial via a sonic sensibility: curating not works, spaces and objects, but their indivisible connections and processes, to reveal their politics through conversations staged in the invisible sound of water telling unreliable tales.

The second chapter considers 'The possibility of resistance and the performance of alternatives'. It contemplates the body and language through working out and dancing and performs alternatives from the speechless materiality of reps and breaths that breach the line. Reading Kathy Acker and Adrian Piper's texts as works, it speculates on how the body in training might bring us to knowledge about language and art beyond the ordinary, beyond critique, but in a resonating sphere, where through creative resistance and an entangled sense we curate without producing normative standards or conventional significance, but engage in participation and the in-between. It does so by working out and dancing, to feel the body in a speechless mode and to practice a solitude and a communality that makes us rethink how we belong together and where we belong.

The third 'Listens across' history, politics, works and texts 'to uncurate knowledge' through a performance off the line. This is a semantic line as well as a historical line, which provides reference and orientation for an objective truth that stays at a distance but oppresses what is local and tacit, feminist and contingent. In response, I involve my body to follow a score of texts and instructions, and listen across disciplinary, gendered, class and other boundaries, to disorder the curatorial frame. Drawing with chalk a white line and troubling it with queerer gestures, on hands and knees, while playing Kate Carr's composition of a river and listening to Ellen Fullman's Long String instrument turning on a muted record player, I reconsider Modernism's absence and negativity as a colonial ideology and arrive at the vibrational presence of a plural sense.

The fourth listens to two pieces, one made with the voice the other with hands: Marguerite Humeau's *Weeds* is in conversation with Manon de Boer's *Think about Wood, Think about Metal*, to reconsider listening as an activity that extends the heard through sound and through the body into actions and a way of knowing from *being with*. Thus, this penultimate chapter presents the second part of the title and links the 'uncuratorial' to a human and more than human body that avoids theory and reference to the canon, but agitates, between listening and sounding, a direct knowing 'With voice and hands'. This knowing stands in resistance to the exclusions of history and lexica, of archives and taxonomies that determine and evidence objective knowledge, generating instead the uncontained and disorderly knowledge of a sonic physical optics that carries an ethical engagement with the work/world.

And finally a fifth chapter on 'Postnormality' does not finish by articulating an end, and does not define an after, but tries to practice repetition without going back and doing again, by going forward … by understanding the pandemic as a troubling of the continuous line, revealing instead a complex simultaneity of now and then, before and after, through which we can deliberately lose our footing and find a groundless ground on which to try alternative possibilities, where the comfort of normality, tied as it is to the causes of the pandemic, has lost its sheen, and we can see its perfidy. This last chapter reflects on Christa Wolf as a double agent, and considers the photographs of Zanele Muholi, which do not show everything but make us participants and responsible for both the visible and the invisible: for what we think we see through our expectations and habits, and for what else is told as marks on bodies, and between work, text and a political history that sound the encounter between 'post' and 'normality'.

Breath 1

Curating politics in the gallery space

recently read two compelling essays in parallel.[1] One was a text by Lina Džuverović and Irene Revell on the unwell and unwilling curator, 'Lots of Shiny Junk at the Art Dump: The Sick and Unwilling Curator';[2] the other was by Boris Groys on 'Politics of Installation',[3] a text that observes on the sick and poorly art work in need of a curator to restore its powers. The first writes about the free labour and unconditional, affective work required to be valued as a 'young', not institutionally secure, curator and the resulting precarity and illness that such an insatiable environment produces: 'One's value lies in one's willingness to bring these gems of ideas and funding like religious offerings to institutions whose operational structures are based precisely on sucking out this kind of enthusiasm for as long as possible.'[4] The second discusses the apparent powerlessness of the artwork that remains unpublicized, unshown, unseen, as a sickness and helplessness to be cured by the curatorial project: 'In order to see it, viewers must be brought to it as

---

[1]This and the next chapter found their starting point in a shorter and more tentative text with their combined title 'Uncurating Politics in the Gallery Space: The Possibility of Resistance and the Performance of Alternatives', written for the *New Literary Observer*: «Неприкосновенный запас», 'Emergency Ration' (2020): 134, edited by Evgeny Bylina, published in Russian only.

[2]Lina Džuverović and Irene Revell, 'Lots of Shiny Junk at the Art Dump: The Sick and Unwilling Curator', *Parse* 9 (Spring 2019). http://parsejournal.com/article/lots-of-shiny-junk-at-the-art-dump-the-sick-and-unwilling-curator/ (accessed 17 November 2020).

[3]Boris Groys, 'The Politics of Installation', *e-flux Journal*, no. 2 (January 2009). https://www.e-flux.com/journal/02/68504/politics-of-installation/ last (accessed 17 November 2020).

[4]Džuverović and Revell, 'Lots of Shiny Junk', online.

visitors are brought to a bed-ridden patient by hospital staff.[5] While Groys critiques this understanding and attitude and sees a potential for resistance in the installation as an autonomous artistic sphere of practice able to reinstate the sovereignty of the artist in her own material organization and work, Džuverović and Revell see a potential resistance in a sense of care and healing: the *curare* of the curator herself, in solidarity and by going slow.

Between the two texts there exists a circle of care that is political in the way that it rethinks the etymological origin of 'curation', reflecting the Roman official in charge of public infrastructure through the assignation of a domiciliary responsibility for mental and physical health, performed in the professional context of art; and that is political in the way that it allows me to consider the colonial heritage of the curatorial frame, its aesthetic economy of exploitation, as a straight line between sugar, cotton, tobacco and contemporary art; and that is political also in the way that it reveals, within the care of curation the antinomy of violence fuelled by the hunger for 'Shiny Junk'.

Together, the two texts open an alternative perspective on curation and the artwork, the curator and the artist, into which as viewers we are tied and made complicit through our engagement with the work, the exhibition. The parallel reading of these texts brings art into view not through the infrastructure of showing, the actual and ideological frame of an exhibition, nor as installation, executed autonomously by the artist, but through the politics of making work and of making the exhibition, understood as the governance of desire and need, and the manipulation of care and how we view work, in communality or as singular viewers. Thus, between them, they write, beyond the concerns of each text, a reappraisal of the ills of curation in a broader sense. And they make visible and thinkable a politics that reaches beyond the particular political concern of the work or the exhibition. What is not a political message, but reveals itself in the way that the artist or curator responds to the condition of making, showing and seeing work: in how they engage in the political economy, history and ideology of the curatorial project and of the institution. This is a politics of organization, of power and of violence, as a violence done to how we move, and look and listen together or alone.

The juxtaposition of these two texts serendipitously unfolds on the problem of artistic and political structures and folds in on notions of care and curation. Together they bring to mind issues of alterity and possibility: how an exhibition/how politics, could be different and differently perceived by

---

[5]Groys, 'Politics of Installation', online.

slowing down, by taking care of all protagonists, human and more than human involved, and by thinking work and the world through its installation, in the predicative: as a process of relationships and relationships in process, rather than as an organization of individuated and finished pieces, that as *Stücke* are always already partial and not a varied entirety, and therefore are unable to remain in process and to resist adaption to the whole – that is, to the curatorial/political, institutional or linguistic frame and organization.[6] Thus curated, works as pieces can only be read through the whole, the institution and the canon: the line that resonates in reverse the value of sugar, cotton and tobacco, lives and deaths, rather than troubling its reading and form. Further, and because of the critical relationship between art/subjectivity as/in pieces, partial and without agency, and curation as the governance of these pieces, the juxtaposition of these two texts helps me consider how curation as a form of care and conversation could represent a form of broader political resistance to a unified and habitual view, and how it could achieve what we now consider impossible: the reorganization of power as a matter of care, working through as yet invisible but plural gestures of interaction and responsibility, off the line, to build a different solidarity. In the context of the gallery space, this implies a solidarity between curators; curators and artists; curators, artists and exhibition visitors, with the work, the institutional architecture, its infrastructure of human and more than human things: generating a different communality of the (art) world that is not governed and legislated but practised, and that presents its asymmetries as part of the artistic process and for debate.

---

[6]Étienne Balibar's mention of the German term *Stücke*, pieces, refers to its use by the Nazis to describe the individuals in the concentration camps, illustrating the linguistic and thus quasi-technological effort of fascism at depersonalization as part of the systemic, ultraobjective violence perpetrated against the Jews. Balibar goes on to articulate its current use in global capitalism and the way it eliminates its superfluous population: those who neither work nor consume, those who do not have the capacity to fulfil the role assigned to them by the system. Applying Balibar's interpretation of *Stücke* articulated in relation to the ultraobjective violence of the Nazi era and global capitalism to the art market and the context of commercial curation reveals art works as pieces, and therefore as partial objects, reduced to a particular, derogative reading and use, unable to reach what else they might be and abandoned if they do not fulfil their role within the curatorial system. The artwork as *Stück* signifies the cut away from the possibility of the work as material in process, to be simply a piece, a *Stück*, not relevant in the context of practice, but only in the context of artistic value, the collection. Thus, art as piece, as *Stück*, is without agency or variability and lacks the possibility to resist and to transform. (Étienne Balibar, *Violence and Civility, On the Limits of Political Philosophy*, trans. G. M. Goshgarian (New York: Columbia University Press, 2015), 69).

Groys identifies the exhibition space as a 'symbolic property of the public',[7] which is therefore assumed as neutral and accessible. According to him it is the space within which the curator as administrator provides the work's justification and explanation. By contrast, the installation signifies the private space of the artist who owes no justification or explanation to the public, who as visitors temporarily inhabit its structures but always according to its rules. For Groys, the visitor to an installation, unlike that of a conventional exhibition, does not singularly go from work to work, but moves within a group of visitors all sharing in the same space made from things in correlation, as a mass of 'viewers' that form communities, which 'resemble those of travellers on a train or airplane'.[8] They are as he terms it 'radically contemporary communities' not based on a common origin or shared past, but emergent from a present sharing of a particular experience. They are transitory, de-territorialized, and circulate in the 'aura of the here and now' of the installation, that is the private realm of the artist, in which we as visitors are 'reterritorialized' and 're-auratized': regaining the aura lost according to Walter Benjamin through mechanical reproduction, in a communal viewing and walking.[9]

For Groys, the 'private' space of the installation depends on the sovereignty of the artist in order for it to become a democratic space, and in turn the artist's sovereignty embodies and thus personalizes the mechanism of power that stands at the beginning of the democratic order, and remains mobilized within it. According to him, it is the installation artist as physical legislator, or caretaker, of this power, and the artistic practice of installation that comes to 'reveal the hidden sovereign dimension of the contemporary democratic order that politics, for the most part, tries to conceal'[10]. However, rather than the potential for a care-full and caring politics of installation, I recognize in this practice of 'unconcealing' an acceptance and mimicry of violence and coercion as the only form art can take and the only form politics can take, to generate a community of the here and now: to be relevant, to be recognizable, to be valuable, to have an aura and a territory. Therefore, while the artwork as installation is not sick anymore, and does not need the curator to bring the audience to the work as to a sick bed, there is no room in this private aesthetics for a different political possibility: one that reaches beyond the order of democracy as a community made from

---

[7]Groys, 'Politics of Installation', online.
[8]Ibid.
[9]Ibid.
[10]Ibid.

violence and dependent on this violence to sustain its form, which can develop into an order of care and care-fullness to human and more than human bodies that find their own.

The audience remains unwell. We are governed by the conceptual and material law-making of the artist and the art institution, which facilitates the install; and we are subject to the violence of the installation as the dynamic of governance and history of the state and of the curatorial, as a colonial and organizing, ordering and taxonomizing, rather than a caring principle, whose violence is concealed by the white walls of the gallery and disguised by its apparent neutrality and accessibility, but whose power is nevertheless part of its aesthetic condition, and generates a political conditioning.

Thus, while the shift from exhibition to installation might 'unconceal', as in reveal, the violence of curation through the reorganization of the conventional exhibition space and its authorship, it remains mobilized within it: it retains its force in the violence of the artist, whose sovereignty frees them to 'curate' their installation, while at the same time determining the rules of freedom, or nonfreedom, that guide and organize the visitors, the distinction is minimal. We might not look at pieces any more, and thus the elements of the work might have re-attained their varied entirety, to be as art and as thing, not partial but connecting. The audience, however, remains a piece, directed in our concorporation as multitude, as a community of mobile difference, through the here and now appearance of the work.[11] Thus, the shift from curation to installation does not per se dispel the violence of curation. It remains within the 'antinomies of the same order', revealed but not resisted.[12] And the political model of democracy that Groys evokes from the ancient

---

[11]In this point I disagree with Groys. The simple fact that the artist resists curation through installation and therefore takes over the governance of space and things does not automatically imply that they reveal and therefore unconceal the hidden sovereign dimension of power, or that this should necessarily lead to a more collaborative, symmetrical and thus caring approach. The installation does not always and in any event unconceal the power of the institution; it can simply represent a continuation and even amplification of that very power through an amalgamation of pieces sublimated to the organization of artistic freedom under whose spell I as visitor am organized and instrumentalized.

[12]In *Violence and Civility*, Étienne Balibar discusses the idea and hope that violence can be eliminated as fundamental to our idea of politics, which is legitimated by this aim of order and control. He suggests that this attempt at controlling violence becomes a force that suppresses the possibility of politics in an infinite circularity between violence and antiviolence, through which politics takes on an antinomic logic, trapped in the imagination of violence and its opposite, unable to resist or find alternatives (Balibar, *Violence and Civility*, 5).

Greeks might be made more personal and visible through the role of the artist, but no less violent, and no alternative can be gleaned.

The visitor-communities might not be forced into a particular understanding of pieces on the wall. Instead, they are forced into a particular participation: in the way they get moved through and mobilized by materials, human and more than human things, that *are* the installation as organized through the sovereign freedom of the artist, who replaces curatorial administration through artistic legislation but is unable to uncurate its logic.

An example of this violence of artistic legislation happens in Janet Cardiff and George Bures Miller's *The Dark Pool* (2009).[13] The installation guides us, six visitors at the time, through a dark and crowded, and by all accounts long-abandoned, artist's studio. Things are piled up on tables and stacked up against walls. From smaller and larger funnels emerge voices that order our present direction through a narration of the past. And so I walk on the given track while my walking and moving triggers interactive devices that start sounds which tell stories about the objects' present, expanding on what we do not see in the dark, and determining my rhythm. The design of the installation and the walking as a community of visitors does not permit multiple paths or a turning around. The dimmed atmosphere and insistent narrations hush dissent and coerce my museological habitus on a certain path, choreographing my viewing and listening possibility. I too am installed in the work, as a moving part, as an interactive element, moving in an arrangement of human and more than human things as pieces.

In this sense and round-about way, I come to think from the idea of the installation as resistance to curatorial interference, disguised as kindly care, to the politics of artistic freedom and the control of the visitor, revealing the Western tension between individual sovereignty and the violence of legislation. Thus, we circulate back to care and care-fullness for the curator and the artist, as well as the visitor, bound up together in the tension between the violence of legislation, organization, sovereign working, architectural infrastructure, material relationships, the possibilities of freedom and the habitus of looking at work/the world. And

---

[13]I wrote about this work, which I experienced at the Oxford Museum of Modern Art, UK, 2009, in rather uncritical admiration in *Listening to Noise and Silence: Hearing the Continuum of Sound* (New York: Bloomsbury, 2010). It has taken me all this time, more than ten years, to understand the violence of this installation, and in fact of a lot of their work, which in its slick über-organization and instruction leaves no room, no breath to think and move another way.

it becomes apparent that the problem lies not in the fact that the 'young curator' is not cared for, has to provide free labour and unconditional, affective work, suffering precarity and illness. That is only a symptom of an oppressive regime, which directs our gaze and our arms, and legs and ears rather than entering into conversation, and whose accessibility reflects my sublimation rather than my voice. I have to remain on the line of the installation plan and its instrumentality, and within the canonical definition of value and sense.

Cardiff and Bures Miller's work uses the apparent neutrality of the gallery, its public accessibility, to commandeer their status as artists, and to establish the work as art work. Their sovereignty is based on my participation but not on dialogue or collaboration. While they have withdrawn themselves from the control of the curator, and thus managed to take care of themselves, they have not extended this care to me as their visitor. And while they dramatize their work, and thus resist curation through the installative, realizing Groys' suggestion and avoiding the violence of control, they do not extend this freedom to me. Instead, their freedom and self-care are dependent on my unfreedom, or what Bonaventure Ndikung terms an 'un-caring', where the care for one or oneself involves the uncaring for another.[14]

For their work to stand as art I must walk their path, and move my arms and my legs to trigger the fragments that as installation I cannot take apart but am forced to perform as a whole. Thus, I become a hostage to their politics that un-cares for me. Never mind the content of the work, which I have long forgotten. What remains is an imprint on my body, that as element of the work feels its power play, and that as element of my life feels the governance of paths, footsteps, movements and actions and how they are curated by the violence of norms and civic design that suppress the possibility of alterity: my own variants and that of others.

In this way, the gallery, the museum, the exhibition space is revealed as the stage for the performance of (art's) politics as a politics of power and coercion. *The Dark Pool* instrumentalizes my viewing, walking and listening and thus confirms rather than challenges or critiques the violence of governance and the legislation of curation. As a deterritorialized group of installation visitors walking through the here and now of the installation, we have no ground from which to unperform this violence: we can refuse to enter the work/the gallery, but once we are in the installation we inevitably and powerlessly perform its form.

---

[14]Bonaventure Soh Bejeng Ndikung, *The Delusions of Care* (Berlin: Archive Books, 2021), 35.

Inhalation: Power lines

Curation's colonial foundation and incredibly purposeful infrastructure houses the apparently purposeless, the playful and the extravagantly unusable, whose resistance to use value and rational sense apparently withdraws it from neoliberal exploitation to express artistic freedom and possibility. It also, however, reveals and plays out the paradox of un-caring and the violence of aesthetic coercion, as the lack of usefulness enables its use within art and determines ours in its creation and legitimation. The artwork and the curator are dependent on the historical and ideological design of the gallery, as architecture and as cultural concept, to legislate the work as piece and to legislate the body of the audience as viewer, in order to give shape and value to a form that resists the same.

The purposelessness of art sets out to defy the line of value financed by lines of exploitation, while at the very same time its purposelessness grants opportunity for the performance of social and financial politics, understood as the governance of care and neglect, to frame the possibility of art through the possibility of the political. Thus, the art work makes a form that remains formless but forms values and orders validity. And the art world, through its own resistance to use value, becomes the stage for neoliberal exploitation, performed as the continuation of the colonial in the curatorial frame, whose operational structures demand quasi-religious fervour and devotion to bring offerings to the machine of purposeless *über-value* and to instrumentalize human and more than human bodies as bodies of work. Its workers and artists, curators and visitors cannot escape the violent politics of order and organization; and the artwork, whatever its content, will be sublimated into this notion of validity and meaning through an ordering along canonical, geographical, economic, colour, gender and other lines. Therefore, political resistance and ultimately the practice of a different politics not tied to the colonial structures of curatorial organization, not tethered to the line, cannot lie, or cannot lie only, in the content of the work but in how it responds to the infrastructure of display: how it reimagines the history and ideologies of the curatorial frame; how it deals with its economy; how it engages, or not, in an ethics of care; and how it enables, or not, the community of practice that makes its processes visible.

Cardiff and Bures Miller's *The Dark Pool* instrumentalizes the gallery and its curatorial convention to authorize and guard the work as work. And it instrumentalizes my walking through an un-caring installation, in which I become a partial element that makes the work technologically viable, forcing my presence into a participation that quite literally makes the work sound and move, light up and remain dark, but leaves me mute and as a piece, a *Stück*. Their work feeds off and reiterates the violence of art and curation, the power play of the display through which I walk to ensure their visibility while sublimating mine. By contrast, Kara Walker's *Fons Americanus* (2020) engages her installative-curatorial position in a different mode and politics. She does not draw on the authority of the gallery to authorize her work, and she does not use her sovereignty to determine mine. Instead, she confronts the gallery and the viewer with their history and present orientation: challenging how we connect to its power of validation, representation and worth and how we move along the historical line to justify its present continuance. Confronted thus, I exist in the possibility of the encounter rather than as the mediator of the work, and so I meet the work in its variability to experience the unconcealment of the institution, of myself, of art and of politics, as a decolonization of a more oppressive form of art and curation that corresponds to an oppressive form of politics.

Fons Americanus is a life-sized fountain that according to Walker was inspired by the Victoria Memorial in front of Buckingham Palace in London and by the sense of water as a dream or a nightmare, in which 'we swim or we sink'. It is a piece 'about oceans and seas traversed fatally', whose traversing it retells through an appropriation of the imperial aesthetic remade from the recyclable materials of cork, soft wood and metal and coated in resin.[15]

It is not so much exhibited by the Tate as it occupies its Turbine Hall, at the very back, beyond the concourse, where Louise Bourgeois' spider sat and Doris Salcedo cracked its concrete floor.[16] It is inevitably in conversation

---

[15]'The *Fons Americanus* is an allegory of the black Atlantic, and really all global water which disastrously connect Africa to America, Europe and economic prosperity', Kara Walker in the documentary video https://www.youtube.com/watch?v=tV_L3fceGNA (accessed 27 December 2021). In this video, Walker also talks about her need to keep a handcrafted feel to the sculpture, which she does by making miniature models of each character by hand, in clay, and by working from hand-drawn sketches, and finally by working again, with her hands and resin, over the robot made sculpture.

[16]Doris Salcedo's work *Sibboleth* was shown at Tate Modern in 2007. It manifests as a gap in the concrete floor, starting as a hairline crack at the doors, and getting ever deeper and wider as it progresses into the space of the Turbine Hall. Representing, according to the artist, 'borders, the experience of immigrants, the experience of segregation, the experience of racial hatred' (*The Times*, 9 October 2007). Seven years prior, for the opening of Tate Modern in 2000, *Maman* the giant, bronze, stainless steel and marble, spider of Louise Bourgeois, was installed in that very place where the crack will get wider

with these works, reflecting too on border lines and segregation, and drawing on their feminine/feminist powers. But it also opens an entirely different space from without the gallery, outside the notion of sculpture, art, installation altogether, where the work narrates a story that confronts the Tate's history and present situation and which confronts us as visitors with how we perceive ourselves in its historico-geographical tale.

This is a tale of exploitation, transportation, lines of money made and lives lost. Walker stages these stories around and inside the fountain's iconic shape, whose diameter stretches almost the whole of the space. In this way, she meets expectations of monuments to the empire in a display of trees with thick nooses, a weeping boy in an oyster shell, sharks, drowning bodies, sailors, nefarious sea captains, a snorkelling swimmer and praying figures animated by the joyful and refreshing rippling and splashing of water that flows from the cut throat and the exposed breasts of the heroine positioned atop. The fountain stages a beautiful disaster, which at first glance and without glasses does not much deviate from its initial inspiration. It is in the *being with* the work and in its confrontation that the details emerge to tell their story that split up normative lines of history and representation and instead perform the indivisibility between art, money, exploitation, death, politics and our ways of viewing work and the world.

Fons Americanus speaks to the outside, and every imperial monument, while addressing the heart of the Western museological and curatorial project and its colonial past. Thus, it does not have to be outside. We will take it outside after experiencing its confrontation. Re-seeing every fountain in its rippling disastrous joy anew, not by erasure, but by superimposing other stories. Pluralizing what we see, opening invisible facets and stories, hidden in the factual discourse and iconic representation of history and of art, whose apparent reliability justifies its exclusions. Revealing consequences and re-seeing connections that perform reorientations and produce alternative realities not along hierarchal lines, but in their breach. Backwards, across the ocean, where sugar comes from, that sustains the authority and power of art, to find allegiance in exploitation on either side of the Atlantic.

The artist describes herself as an unreliable narrator.[17] I sense her story in the water gently splashing from the fountain, fluid, not tied to historical

---

and deeper to show the negative space of absence and non-belonging, and where in 2020 the fountain of Kara Walker showed the fatal consequences of colonial lines.

[17]Reference in video at https://www.youtube.com/watch?v=tV_L3fceGNA (accessed 27 December 2021).

facts, but opening the present from its plural memory. Intoned by water, hers is an inaudible narrative voice that mingles with the voices of the visitors and the murmurs of the architecture to define the Turbine Hall in a different tacicity: as invisible and indivisible materiality and sense in whose plural knowledge we come to be entangled. Through this entanglement, the work uncurates the politics of art and of the world and confronts my own position without instrumentalizing it. Instead, the voice as water tends to the material and forms the figures, and forms them in their joy and trauma, to converse with the past in the present, and on a fluid path. In this way, it pluralizes the imagination of slavery and exploitation in which we take part and are made responsible.

As artist curating her installation, Walker's care manifests in this confrontation between history, representation and responsibility. Her care-fullness is not benign but accountable to plural stories not yet told. It unconceals the un-caring of the institution, of politics and of art, by practising her sovereignty not as unaccountable power *over* but as a responsibility *for*. Thus, she produces a work that disables a comprehensive gaze but shows the complexity of participation and entanglement through confrontation and the need to see at the fountain's depth, at its back and behind, a new perception of myself and of the institution.[18]

---

[18]Here Maurice Merleau-Ponty's notion of depth helps to articulate a radical position from which perception can re-orientate itself. Merleau-Ponty explains this depth as the back and behind of things, which according to him is the dimension of the hidden and the simultaneous, where the world surrounds me. It is the place which I cannot see but from which I see, and thus from which things attain their distinction for me. This invisible place is at once the place of my perception and it is the place through which I come to understand the incompleteness of the seen through my effort of deduction, by which in judgement I complete what is hidden, which is what I cannot see behind the table, behind the chair: synthesizing viewpoints and working from prior knowledge to get to a total view. This, as Sara Ahmed clarifies, is the point of orientation, which reveals perception as ideological, a question of how near or far we are in our assumptions of the seen, and how we choose to complete the image (Maurice Merleau-Ponty, *The Visible and the Invisible*, trans. Alphonso Lingis, ed. Claude Lefort (Evanston, IL: Northwestern University Press, 1968), 220; Sara Ahmed, 'Orientation Matters', in *New Materialism, Ontology, Agency, and Politics*, ed. Diana Coole and Samantha Frost (London: Duke University Press, 2010), 234–5).

However, according to Merleau-Ponty, this depth is also *openness*. I read this openness, through the sonic, as an access point to the dimension of the invisible, from where I see but cannot see myself, but gain, listening a different sense: the sense of my complicity and responsibility. Since in sound there is no back and no behind. Everything sounds simultaneously and, while I cannot see myself seeing, I am audible to myself hearing. Thus, sound unconceals relationships and visual exclusions and remeasures their

From here, and going back to Džuverović and Revell's concern for the young and precarious curator trapped in the *über-value* machine of art by her own hope for sustainable employment and recognition, we could rethink the role of the curator, as well as the sovereignty of artistic production, within a notion of such care-fullness. We could come to appreciate freedom as inextricably linked to responsibility and ethics, and thus to the responsibility for 'response-ability', Donna Haraway's ecology of practice that cultivates a collective from the ability to respond: from the contingent relating between human and more than human bodies with all voices audible.[19] Such a mutual audibility is needed to take care of and make room for participation as co-production that is not organized but is building and taking apart together. In this way, the curator does not just select and determine how to organize and thus legislate the appearance and value of a work. Instead, 'the labour involved in curating may take a turn and begin to operate in the realm of "the curatorial," which, depending on how one understands it, could be imagined as an arena in which it is possible to rethink ways of being, working with others, thinking about methods and processes rather than outputs'.[20] And where equally, the artist does not install their own curatorial authority to outperform the power of the curator, performing an aesthetic supremacy and coercion through instrumentalization, but works with complex relationships and in responsible entanglements between things human and more than human, in order to *be with* and *work with*, slowly and with care, so we might see the depth of the work, that which we cannot see in a straight gaze, but which shows us ourselves and creates a confrontation rather than a work.

For care to effect a sustained transformation rather than erase itself in the antinomy of violence, of art and of the institution, it needs to stage an entanglement and confrontation that avoids un-caring as the prize for care. Such care is powerfully performed in Walker's work: in how her fountain disables a comprehensive, grasping gaze but shows the complexity of empire and exploitation through entanglement and confrontation at its back. How it makes me responsible for my perception: for how I understand the fountain, how I understand its water as troubling of historical facts through the polyphony of narrations, from breasts and throats cut and eyes crying. The installation shot might pretend the possibility to grasp the work,

---

deductions to show us the norms of our orientations while also providing the possibility to unform them, generating a different *openness*.
[19]Donna Haraway, *Staying with the Trouble: Making Kin in the Chthulucene* (Durham, NC: Duke University Press, 2019), 34.
[20]Džuverović and Revell, 'Lots of Shiny Junk', online.

to hold it in our gaze and thus to realign it with the iconography of the museum as a monument and sculptural form, continuing a line of forms. But rather than looking *at*, but seeing *with* the work, from its depth, it opens a different relationship. From our individual positions, we can never see all those drowned and drowning, literally and politically. Therefore, we have to walk around and explore what we cannot see when we see 'this' or 'that', so we might recognize what emerges from their connection and through our indivisibility and come to appreciate what we cannot account for from over there at an objective distance, but have to embrace close up and intimate, in an objectivity of responsibility and care. To sense rather than see its story, whose invisible connections we have to conjure ourselves, from the splashing narration of the water flowing from the cut throat that is not able to speak, but whose sound ties me into the work, as it reveals in the seeming iconography of the empire its blind spots, its depth, the things that are invisible but determine its form.

Exhalation: Going slow

Džuverović and Revell ask whether to cure the sickness of curation we can hold a space for not doing, for slowing down, for care and solidarity[21] – to stand outside the insatiable demands of cultural production while still working within it. With them I ask whether in resistance to the violence of curation and the coercion of the installation, we can find a different pace while remaining relevant. That is a pace that is not necessarily slower but walks in and from different directions and with a different gait, and thus confronts the institution with its colonial economy and violent cravings and questions its constant need for new offerings, by generating alternative possibilities.

Care-full work and careful curation, as a tending to the human and more than human protagonists of art, does not have to make the work less relevant, less pertinent or contemporary, which is one of the fears of going slow and cultivating a caring environment: to lose one's edge and the hunger that contemporary markets and institutions strive on and demand. Instead, by slowing down, the curatorial project might be able to pluralize and find new imaginations for relevance and quality, not as a line of contemporaneity, but as a diffuse and plural range of co-productions: as an expansive and inclusive possibility of joint activity and *working with*.

---

[21]Ibid.

It might be less spectacular, in a visually determined and recognizable way. The work might disavow its own image: the installation shot and the catalogue iconography, that confer its individuated status and singular value.[22] It might refuse representation and a singular authorship and might instead favour collaborative 'digging and gardening' that create, from the dark and invisible material at its depth and between the seen, what the work is.[23]

While this might rob the work/the exhibition of its value as a graspable thing that in its purposelessness can feed the purpose of finance and the violent hunger of curating and collecting and while therefore the work might have less meaning and value in relation to a conventional curatorial infrastructure, its political economy of authorship and representation, it might generate critical value through confrontation. And while this might demand a different form of engagement – inviting a digging and tending to the material at its depth, from blind spots and in co-laboration – it might produce a more open and plural sense from the sensorial. Such a sense might tend to and care for the invisible in-between rather than visualize it through an infrastructural reference and in evidence of a line. Thus, it

---

[22]'Installative Kunst kann, wie ich meine, nicht hinreichend durch den zumeist eigentlich sterilen Installation shot, so nennt man nicht nur Ausstellungsfotos, sondern mittlerweile eben auch photographische Dokumentationen installativer Werke, wiedergegeben werden … weil für ihre Erfahrung die Differenz zum Bild, die dritte Dimension, wesentlich ist' (Juliane Rebentisch, *Ästhetik der Installation* (Germany: Edition Suhrkamp, 2003), 18).

'Installation art, can, in my opinion, not be adequately represented through the installation shot, which is the name given currently not only to exhibition photographs, but also to the photographic documentation of installative works, (…) because the difference to the image, the third dimension, is important for the experience of an installation' (author's translation). This third dimension is the collective of human and more than human bodies that are at once an installation's material and its protagonists. It is from their between, in a relational performance, that the installation is produced. Therefore, and in confirmation and elaboration on Juliane Rebentisch's assertion on the installation shot's inability to capture this dimension, the installation is not simply in excess of the image, and the image is not simply unable to capture the installation; moreover, the installation as a political imagination of curation in communal practice disavows the ability to capture art in the value format of an individuated piece.

[23]Inspired by Rosi Braidotti's ideas on philosophy 'a sort of intellectual landscape gardening' of an embodied mind (*Nomadic Subjects, Embodiment and Sexual Difference in Contemporary Feminist Theory*, 2nd edn (New York: Columbia University Press, 2011), 46), in *The Political Possibility of Sound*, I suggest that 'we might have to go gardening, digging and turning the earth to understand the world instead' (Salomé Voegelin, *The Political Possibility of Sound* (New York: Bloomsbury, 2018), 153). And thus, we might have to garden, to dig and turn the earth, the ground, to understand the work.

might generate the understanding of a work in conversation: formless, unfolding in our *being with*; promoting a sensorial sense and durational experience that is close up and responsible; and, rather than appreciative of the recognizable, is productive instead of response-ability.

In this sense, this critical slowness is not a leaning back into privilege and certainty, of what art is and what the work is, enabled by economic security and professional standing of the artist or the curator. It is not so much a slowing down as a purposeful inefficiency: a going sideways and beside itself rather than charting a straight and purposeful line. It is therefore not less rigorous or less engaged, but pursues practice along different lines that are plural, material and ephemeral, that have no clear aim and outcome, and point to their in-between rather than at a finished work. It is not a slow time but a slow, or maybe thick, materiality and process, that unfolds in a complex relationality *with*, rather than in evidence *of*.

Therefore, going slow as in walking with the work from and in many directions, the art work, exhibited or installed, disavows legislation in favour of confrontation: confronting us with the plural possibility of art, of politics and of ourselves and triggering entanglement rather than a viewing. Such a going slow does not simplify or take time; instead, it brings the work into a different proximity, and it does not only 'slow down' the curatorial process, but also pluralizes and thickens the visitor's experience.

Instead of seeing a finished, 'shiny' work, they will have to enter its invisible duration, to come and experience it in its process of unfolding, where it becomes a *work with*: with time, with other viewers, with the artist, with the curator, with the material, with the infrastructure, with politics, with the everyday and so on, rather than in its immediate disguise as art. In this way, the art work represents not a designed object but the meeting ground of artist, curator and visitor, who might all experience similar professional and private tensions of hope and precarity to that of the young curator considered by Džuverović and Revell.

Because, not only curation, but most contemporary professional structures operate on the basis of 'sucking out' enthusiasm for little money from those most desperate and precarious, young or old. The new curator is the nurse or the teacher, who will do overtime for little or no money because of the passion for her cause and her unwillingness to leave the sick and those in need of care, or to leave behind those who go without educational opportunities. However, the sick artwork, which according to Groys is left in the hands of a curatorial system that treats it until it is unwell and has lost all autonomy and from whose apparent illness the curatorial system gets its legitimacy by perfidy in the first place, needs a different form of care. It is not the art work but its curatorial frame that needs attention: a care-full curatorial project, rather than confirming the sickness of the work and the myth of speed and seemingly effortless and endless delivery of shiny productions to cure it, could reveal the politics of abuse at an infrastructural level. Not through representation, as a political art, but as experience, from the politics of art. Thus, instead of showing the finished and accomplished work, bedazzling the visitor with the perfection and ambiguous clarity of the artist and curator, normalizing abuse and ill health through their apparent ease of achievement and success, it is in the struggle, the process, the *doing with* of art as joint gardening, digging and planting, that we might get to recognize each other in our shared condition. In this way, we might come to join in the slow process of doing something care-fully, and art might come to be a process of solidarity in which sovereignty does not stand for wilful autonomy and the right to determine how others move, look and hear, but as a responsibility towards the other: to look out for, listen to and move towards. This might mean abandoning the existing value and judgement of the 'good art work' in favour of a strong process, which in its value and effect might remain speechless and inarticulate, but nevertheless rigorous and felt. Such a curatorial frame might not deliver works to the insatiable art machine and its financial profiteurs, but it might bring to the imagination and thus to possibility a politics of care, solidarity and slowing down, within and without the (art) world.

The gallery space is a micro-cosmos of the political space. It carries, and even accentuates in its own performative sphere, the same violence and 'obscure transparency of the democratic order'.[24] Therefore, if we are intent on inserting care, care-fullness and equity into the democratic order, we might as well start with the practice of curation, the curatorial and the curator and aim to *uncurate* in order to come to a contemporary *curare* as a care that understands the correlation of freedom and sovereignty with responsibility; that can slow down and be inefficient; and that can appreciate the communities it creates for their potential to rethink how we work and live together within and beyond the gallery in the world understood as an installation of power, violence, desire and hope of young curators, who as young workers of any profession, try to fend off precarity to retain mental and physical health and a sense of self-worth.

Thus, from walking from work to work on the curator-designed but 'public' path of the gallery, and further, from the inhabiting of the 'private' space of the installation, organized by the artist's sovereign authorship, we come to co-elaborate in *uncurating*, as an untethering of the curatorial

---

[24]Groys, 'Politics of Installation', online.

chronology and canonical frame: mixing public and private spheres to build and take the work apart together and disavow the exploited value of purposelessness in a doing that is a material practice, guided by artistic thinking and working through the relationship between matter, subject, art and work/world rather than its history.

Such an approach has gendered tensions as it brings preconceptions of the private, the domestic and notions of care into the public realm of art/ the world, reconfiguring its authority; and it presents a decolonial potential in that it disavows recognition, habits, preset values and hierarchies in favour of a here and now – that is, as Groys's airplane travellers, without a common, referenceable origin but a present shared experience and thus with a future that can hold their plurality – that can at last imagine 'the principle of radical democracy as the power of anyone at all'.[25]

At this point, these ideas remain speculative and in progress. But I feel it there in Kara Walker's work, in how her fountain disables a comprehensive gaze but creates entanglements through confrontation. And I sense it also in the ghosts of earlier works performing the Turbine Hall: this sense of critical but caring closeness and non-coercive participation is conjured in the conceptual outlines and affective potential of Louise Bourgeois' *Maman* and Doris Salcedo's *Sibboleth*. All three works do not show us a total form and do not instrumentalize our viewership in a staged participation, but agitate process and combination. They at least seem to know we are there and care for our position in their process and vis-à-vis the process of the institution. That is how I recognize their criticality, not through the themes only, but in how they agitate the curatorial infrastructure and convention, its history and present practice, and how they confront their viewers to help them see themselves at the depth, in the invisible back and behind of the work, to hear an *openness*.[26]

They remain works and exhibitions: recognizable, with a title, a press release, and wall text. But they offer a way to think the possibility of resistance and the performance of alternatives, to come to the possibility of a political process from the artistic process of the in-between: to unperform the violence of art and of politics through a care-full practice of uncurating that does not negate actuality but practices its possibilities.

---

[25]Étienne Balibar, *Equaliberty* (London: Duke University Press, 2014), 297.
[26]This is Merleau-Ponty's *openness,* which is sensed at the place of his *depth*: the back and behind of things, which we cannot see but which according to him is the dimension of the hidden and the simultaneous, where the world surrounds me. It is the place which I cannot see but from which I see, and thus from which things open themselves to me. (Merleau-Ponty, *Visible and the Invisible*, 220).

Breath 2

The possibility of resistance and the performance of alternatives

To practise uncurating as possibility rather than as negation, I need to know what enables its sensibility and care: what curatorial practice can fulfil the task of bringing care-fullness into the realm of art/politics, mixing the governance of the private and the public, slowing down and becoming purposefully inefficient in the face of the relentless productivity demanded by cultural industries? To work, as I articulate it in the previous chapter, not on a historical foundation, but sideways and beside the line, pluralizing art/world expectations and engaging in materiality and process rather than in evidence and exploitation. Abandoning the *über-value* of the apparently purposeless without losing the relevance of the speechless, the ambiguous and what can as yet not be understood or make itself heard within the value of financial function, and dispersing an existing democratic order that conceals what art reveals in the sovereignty of the artist: the violence of legislation and a shared view. In other words, what are the means by which to trouble and interrupt arts relationship to a history based on exploitation and ill health? What is the work that is not itself part of the cycle of exploitation, that does not abuse either artist, curator, visitor or more than human protagonists?

Or to formulate this question differently: how can the shared remain plural, responsible, care-full and response-able – including also what normally remains unseen and unheard; delivered not on a 'fast-moving (art) world conveyor belt',[1] but in the slow and thick duration of an ethics of participation that hears the apparently unrecognizable and unintelligible in its own voice? To tend to this question and make a proposition that tries to address the work/world as process and as a sphere of responsibility and care, I will turn with Kathy Acker to the practice of working out, to lifting weights as a curation of the body that does not build an ideal form but disrupts language in a speechless act of resistance that sets 'AGAINST ORDINARY LANGUAGE: THE LANGUAGE OF THE BODY' (1993). And I will consider Adrian Piper's 'GET DOWN PARTY. TOGETHER', her *Funk Lessons* produced between 1982 and 1984, and written about in 'Notes on Funk I-II//1985/83', to bring dancing, as a critical collective activity, into the discourse of curation.

I read across notes on Funk and bodybuilding as performances of the body and of culture rather than as texts. Reading across both texts as works, I experience them not in the particularity of bodybuilding or of Funk, themes that tie them to their particular time and geographical location, and to a postmodern notion of art and the everyday. Instead, I read them to imagine how we can work with material and our own materialization to resist the violence of lines, those of language, of reference and of curation, in a simultaneous now.[2] Doing so I hope to find, in a speechless practice that unperforms the body and language, alternative possibilities to the conventions of an organized art/world.

Kathy Acker has been working out. At the time of writing 'Against ordinary Language: The Language of the Body', she would have been doing bodybuilding for ten years and seriously for almost five of them. And for the past few of those five she had, so she says, been trying to write about it. To write about bodybuilding from its experience. But she failed. She deliberates on this failure as a resistance of the body to find articulation in conventional language and considers working out to reveal a negative space of no language, where articulation is reduced to numbers, a few nouns and verbs: 'Sets', 'squats', 'reps', 'do', 'fail', and 'meaning occurs, if at all, only at the edge of its becoming lost.'[3]

---

[1]Džuverović and Revell, 'Lots of Shiny Junk', online.
[2]By not engaging in the works original postmodern context I do not deny that connection and particularity, but hope to underline their enduring relevance of avoiding language when seeking to resist straight lines.
[3]Kathy Acker, 'Against Ordinary Language: The Language of the Body', in *The Last Sex: Feminism and Outlaw Bodies*, ed. Arthur Kroker and Marilouise Kroker (Basingstoke, UK: MacMillan, 1993, 21).

Thus, she describes the space of the workout as a crossing into a nonverbal sphere that is complex and rich, whose experience breaches syntax and instead materializes in a speechless, wordless register. Contemplating this breach of language by the body in training, she suggests that it is only from the negative geography of language and its own implicit failure that bodybuilding can be described. She initiates such a description from the body in a process of repetition, 'the same controlled gestures with the same weights, the same reps, … the same breath patterns.'[4]

These repetitions perform a cycle of breaking down and building up:[5] 'As soon as I can accomplish a certain task, so much weight for so many reps during a certain time span, I must always increase one aspect of this equation, weights reps or intensity, so that I can again come to failure.'[6] Her workouts break muscles to build them, not to hurt the body, but to shock it into growth. However, this growing is set against the body's own unstoppable decay, its vulnerability and movement towards death. And so, every growth is also a failure, that motivates and necessitates the next training that will inevitably also fail. This process of repeated failure remains outside ordinary language since, in this circle of breaking and growing tempered by the inevitability of death, language becomes purposeless in relation to the semantic, but purposeful in relation to the body, forming a different meaning from counting and breathing: 'Each number equals one inhalation and one exhalation.'[7]

I understand this language of breath and repetition, which does not mean semantically but leads the body to its physical sense, as a creative resistance to knowing *about* in favour of a knowing *from*: from practice, from the body, close up and in training/in process.[8] Creating the knowledge of its own material, breaking and building, putting together and taking apart.

Ultimately, it is the failure to control the body wherein the fascination of bodybuilding for Acker lies. For it is in the unexpected and the

---

[4]Ibid., 26.
[5]This is repetition not as repeatability in the scientific sense, performing the confirmation of a previous outcome: doing the same to achieve the same and thereby conferring trust and validity. Instead, this repetition performs unrepeatability, unreliability, proving that nothing can ever be the same.
[6]Ibid., 22.
[7]Ibid., 26.
[8]This body in training meets Julia Kristeva's body in process, on trial, that is mobile and remains signifying but never a signified (Julia Kristeva, *Revolution in Poetic Language* (New York: Columbia University Press, 1984)).

uncontrollable of the body in training, its unreliability and its potential to change, set within a regime of control and repetition, and its reduced language, where she meets what she cannot know and therefore speak about in ordinary language, the body itself: its breath, its matter, felt in repetitive movements and finally in its failure.[9]

But where does this body, building its own sense of self in failure meet curation, and how does it relate to its politics?

By describing the building of the body as revealing unreliability, chance and change, Acker manages to undo the instrumentalization of the body in language and offers us access to its material self. Through her focus on the control of the body working out, and its subsequent failure to be worked out, she meets the body in how it cannot be known in language and its legislation of sense. Because, and maybe paradoxically, the working out considered from the body in its speechlessness does not reveal an ideal form, individuated and perfect, but a fragile materiality in process. Thus, her negotiation of building a form through repetition, breath and failure takes the body off the line of progress and the semantic and breaks it into a complex and contingent experience: 'to come face to face with chaos, with my own failure or a form of death', practising the body in its own disorder, where it is seen as unwell and ill-disposed.[10] From the negative geography of language, where breath and meaning coincide on the count of a reduced speech, she uncurates the body to know it in practice rather than through the iconography of its individuated shape.

Through bodybuilding's resistance to semantic sense and the body's failure to reach a total and ideal form, she practises the undoing of language, as an undoing of the infrastructure of meaning and validity. The resistance of weights performed in repetition brings us to a resistance to ordinary language, in favour of a physical, tacit and contingent knowledge that enables the possibility of the unexpected and the disordered: that which is

---

[9]In this point Acker also meets Judith Butler who too declares it impossible to write about the body, and who too declares it language's fault, not the body's. Her solution is not practice, however, but the unconscious, which I read as the imagination and our thinking beyond language through the body's own signifiers:

> Everytime I write about the body, the writing ends up being about language. This is not because I think the body is reducible to language; it is not. Language emerges from the body, constituting an emission of sorts. The body is that upon which language falters, and the body carries its own signs, its own signifiers, in ways that remain largely unconscious. (Judith Butler, *Bodies That Matter: On the Discursive Limits of Sex* (New York: Routledge, 1993), ix).

[10]Acker, 'Against Ordinary Language', 26.

not semantically right, but true in the performance of language's negative; that which does not speak on the line, through reference and in evidence but through breath as the gap between words that count the body in its wordless repetitions.

When a bodybuilder is counting, he or she is counting his or her own breath.[11]

She cannot write the body, she has to practise it, again and again, but never the same. To break, through repetition, the sense of a conventional body and of conventional language and the illusion of a perfect form. Building her body, she practises chaos and a different meaning, which is disordered and plural and which confronts the distance of objectivity, the iconography of a perfect body, with its speechless, fragile and transforming materiality, close up, in its depth, which remains invisible, a matter of this very practice.

Following Acker to our aim of resisting both bodily and curatorial norms and their legislation, we cannot write conventional language either and cannot work in a conventional curatorial frame as they will inevitably get us to the form rather than to the formless and the disordered. Instead, we have to breach the syntax of language and of the curatorial. We have to work through repetition and breath to find a sense on the body, beside the line in its own chaos: where it fails to form but confronts us with its unreliable narration and change.

Further more, to reach this level of resistance to norms and the perfection of forms, not simply as a solitary and isolated act of speechless repetition, which could find form as a private and singular spiritual totality, we have to do our reps together, we have to breathe together: performing the troubling of language, and bodies, and materiality together. Not to create a harmonious sphere, but to make meaning a matter of practice, of the unexpected and the unreliable of human and more than human bodies in their disorder together, to work through confrontation and conversation, and reveal ourselves to ourselves at reality's speechless depth, where language ceases to communicate and we have to move together, dancing and singing, the work and the world, to think together as in an embodied philosophy.[12]

---

[11]Ibid., 25.

[12]This dancing and singing to communicate at reality's speechless depth, overlaps with Rosi Braidotti's ideas on philosophy as 'a sort of intellectual landscape gardening' of an embodied mind, which I mention in the chapter above in relation to curation. Here it helps

The critical collective energy of 'GET DOWN PARTY. TOGETHER', Adrian Piper's work *Funk Lessons* produced between 1982 and 1984, can help us to imagine and perform this physical contemplation. Piper's lessons confront willing as well as unwitting participants with the notion of collectivity by making them a dancing/listening group to a music associated with a particular social and cultural milieu. In her essay 'Notes on Funk I-II//1985/83', Piper describes the work as a staging of collaborative dance lessons with larger and smaller groups, making them listen and move to Funk. She introduces Funk as a 'language of interpersonal communication and collective self-expression that has its origins in African tribal music and dance and is the result of the increasing interest of contemporary black musicians and the populace in those sources elicited by the civil rights movement of the 1960s and early 1970s'.[13] She differentiates Funk from other social dance forms, and particularly from white Western genres by stressing its collective and participatory role in Black working-class culture, not as a spectacle but as a participatory expression that is integrated in daily life: 'The concern is not how spectacular anyone looks but rather how completely everyone participates in a collectively shared, enjoyable experience.'[14]

Her *Funk Lessons* take this aim of enjoyment and a quotidian collectivity outside of its cultural origin and practise it across race and class identifications, using the collective learning of its steps and rhythms as a form of physical entrainment and participation in the broader cultural and political communication of the music and its socio-political expression. She talks of the intense reactions of joy but also of anxiety, condescension and even anger that some of her interventions provoked and addresses the care-full and supportive environment needed to deal with this physical and auditory learning: to be able to sympathetically confront the issues that arise in the collective performance of a particular cultural and material knowledge.

Her work encourages, through a collective listening and moving, a bodily understanding of music from a Black working-class culture. It operates performance as a form of cultural pedagogy and communication, and curates a process of *caring with* and *being with* the other not vis-à-vis an artwork *or* an installation, but in the process of production: speechless,

---

me to imagine dancing and singing as an embodied philosophy that thinks not through reference but through bodies touching and the in-between (*Nomadic Subjects*, 46).
[13]Adrian Piper, 'Notes on Funk I-II//1985/83', in *Participation Documents of Contemporary Art*, ed. Claire Bishop (Cambridge, MA: MIT Press, 2006), 130.
[14]Ibid.

in anger, resentment and joy. Thus, she curates a multisensory experience of a formless work, whose significance is produced through movement and sound and whose meaning unfolds between bodies in their mobile difference: not by creating an exact reproduction or cultural appropriation and not by insisting on an authentic Funk, but through the performance of our difference so I might see myself in *relation to*.

Piper, as initiator and organizer guides the work. Her text confers authority to her interpretation. However, as a collective performing, the project proposes at least the possibility of a care-full curating as a curatorial project that is committed to the temporary community of curator, artist and audience and that engages them not in a project of justification and legislation, but in a process of confrontation and participation. Piper's work facilitates the communality of listening and dancing to work in the in-between where we do not see but feel the work in its relationality and connecting logic: rebounding different images that do not represent and categorize but generate a care-full *being with*.

> The experiences of sharing, commonality and self-transcendence turn out to be more intense and significant in some ways than the postmodernist categories most of us art-types bring to aesthetic experience.[15]

What is performed is not Funk as a cultural and musical genre or socio-political expression, but the in-between: the between of cultures and aesthetico-political identities. Rebounding mobile difference and practising speechlessness together rather than translating it through a postmodern vocabulary, understood as a vocabulary that defers and de-aligns sense, but ultimately realigns meaning in relation to a linguistic paradigm and its referential frame.

In this way, Piper's work tends to the gaps, to the inarticulate and speechless differences out of which exclusion, class prejudice and racism can grow. It does not realign and bridge these gaps and differences, but performs them, on the body, between bodies, dancing – to find a different sense and a radical solidarity that does not lie in similarity and cultural/political nearness, but in the plural and unreliable narratives of a singing and dancing subjectivity that understands itself through practice and in its contingent relationships with human and more than human bodies.

---

[15]Ibid., 134.

This does not mean eradicating tensions and conflict, or disregarding difference, prejudice or even hate. This is not a performance of sameness or of reconciliation, but of the dimensionality of our difference, which is indivisible and formless. In this sense, the work enables us to perform our participation because of our differing: bringing it to the body, dancing and listening, rather than assuming it as a representation, as an image-able and write-able thing. This means not pushing the difference onto the other but owning it in ourselves. It is the performance of what Étienne Balibar terms an '"internal multiplicity," all *différence* in the self [the "us"] and its others without which no self could exist'.[16]

This internal multiplicity is the body's material multiplicity that is not seen, but is felt in the richness of the experience of the body building itself through reps and breaths, and coming to itself not as an individuated, perfect form but through moving and dancing together, as a changing and transforming body, emerging through its own difference to itself, plural and beyond ordinary language.

From this practice of internal difference, through working out and dancing, we come to understand the work/world relationally and on our body. This bodily knowledge is tacit and complicit. It is a knowledge *with* that speaks in the negative geography of language. Thus, it does not articulate knowledge about the world/the work but from the body with the work/world, generated by their encounter and revelatory about what it produces through the articulation of breaths and hums, songs and bodies moving.

From this entangled position and relational knowledge, we come to see the inevitable failure of curation when it tries to control our gaze and our bodies within its scheme; when it insists to show us work; and when it coerces us to move to its design. By contrast, the body dancing and working out unconceals the violence of legislation, artistic and political, that manifests as the making of singular lines of judgement and justification. It uncurates it in creative resistance by stepping onto these lines, defying the need for order and performing chaos from their in-between. Here we can practise curation as uncuration. As a composing of relational spheres, untethered from historical lines and from conventional language, practised instead by flesh and material bodies in entanglement and confrontation, deliberately stepping on gaps and sliding on uneven surfaces.

---

[16]Balibar, *Violence and Civility*, 61, 69–70.

Inhalation: Sonic volumes

Lines are drawn by history, finance, architecture, artefacts and a disciplinary thinking. They perform monumentality, authority, taste and quality. But they are resisted by the body working out and dancing: speechlessly performing, between human and more than human bodies, in reps and breaths counting, through hums and murmurs, the work and the world in its voluminous dimensionality, made from diffuse vibrations and the indivisibility of human and more than human things.

I experience this voluminous dimensionality and its relational materialization in listening. Sound generates a sonic sphere: a viscous expanse, where we hear not 'this' or 'that', individuated flesh and material bodies, defined by their outline and name, at a distance and different. Instead, sounding human and more than human bodies perform their indivisibility: their sounds meet and materialize together, and representational language is transformed through a shared but formless space and on the body in training and dancing and in its failure to make a certain form.

Sound does not create a space but a generative and reciprocal volume that materializes invisibly the possibility of my working out and dancing body in entanglement and correlation with other human and more than human things. This sonic volume is relational. Thus, it is always already collective, in that it disables the notion of a singular view as well as of a view onto the singular. Instead, it promotes experience as a connecting generativity: producing actuality as the possibility of plural interactions and the reality of indivisibility and stressing the responsibility and the need for response-ability to all that sounds within this sphere.

As sound and as sonic concept, this volume is not defined by architectural and infrastructural delineations, 'here' or 'there'. Instead, it is sensed as invisible materializations, simultaneity and radical porosity that breaches the visual frame through its resistance to forms and their divisibility. In this context of plural and indivisible interactions, the exhibition space, the gallery or the concert hall cannot enable representation and legibility. Sound does not exhibit objects and it does not organize subjects, directing their gaze. Instead, it delivers a fuzzy connectivity of human and more than human bodies, touching and being touched invisibly and from a distance, by the indivisibility of their simultaneous sonic expanse. Thus, it offers a view on plural inter-activities of which legislation, infrastructure and architecture, walls and doors, floors and ceilings, become part but not defining.

This dimensionality is not entered but co-produced. I cannot experience it and cannot experience myself without *being in/with*. It is the depth, at the back of and behind the visible, which reveals its possibilities and within which my orientation becomes apparent to myself.[17] Here I sense more than understand my being as always already a *being with* and orientated. And from here I become responsible for my view and able to transform its gaze through listening as the simultaneity of myself with others.

This fuzzy dimensionality is not efficient. It is not fast and linear, but thick and viscous. It generates a diffuse expanse that is plural and expanding and does not progress into a form but lingers in relationships. I conceive the going slow, which is proposed as a critical resistance to the exploitation of curation by Džuverović and Revell in their essay 'Lots of Shiny Junk at the Art Dump: The Sick and Unwilling Curator' discussed in the previous chapter, not as a linear slowness but as an inefficiency: a production of detours and off-track movements that in themselves are not slow but slow down the line and its formation by going another way and getting lost in the possible.

Sound makes this invisible dimensionality, its critical inefficiency and resistance to representation, accessible as in thinkable. It reveals the work and the world through relational materializations that resist linguistic description and the artistic/political governance of lines. Thus, it offers a sense from which to re-imagine the violence of representation and definition, in art and in politics, through the breath of a contingent rhythm that counts the body as material, in the gaps between words, rather than as name and in evidence. In this way, sound shows the connection of art and politics, not through its subject, as a political art, and not through a historical grand narrative, as a political ontology, but through concurrent efforts of control, as the politics of art: how the curatorial project maps and instrumentalizes my walking and viewing and how it legislates the interpretative effort in its infrastructure of meaning and sense. From here,

---

[17]This depth is articulated via Maurice Merleau-Ponty's notion of depth, his dimension of the hidden and the simultaneous, at the back and behind, where the world surrounds me looking. It is the place which I cannot see but from which I look, and thus from which things attain their distinction for me. This invisible place is at once the place of my perception and it is the place through which I come to understand the incompleteness of the seen which I complete through my effort of deduction, revealing the fiction of the seen and my cultural investment. Thus it is, as Sara Ahmed clarifies, the point of orientation, which is an 'effect of proximities': of what appears near and relevant or what appears far and without meaning, and what thus effects how I complete my view (Merleau-Ponty, *Visible and the Invisible*, 220; Ahmed, 'Orientation Matters', 234–5).

sound enables a creative resistance to both art and politics through our bodies not viewing and activating the work, but working out and dancing, to break the line and resist legibility and ordinary language from the body as formless but connecting form, materializing meaning as sense and taking responsibility.

Sound produces neither a space nor a work, and it does not produce bodies, neither flesh nor material. Instead, it creates volumes and relationalities: 'triggering an understanding of the exhibition space (and of the world), not as a construction of walls, floors and ceilings, windows and doors, but as a dimensionality that has a capacity: the capacity of the work and the capacity of our experience of it'.[18] In the gallery as such a voluminous sphere, we perform the indivisibility of art and politics not through themes and representation, but through our performance of their interdependency and thus of our complicity: how my footsteps, handshakes, breath and murmur are coexistent and in conversation with a curatorial project whose politics of justification and legislation holds the means to separate and order things as forms and to control how we move between them. By contrast, listening I do not see forms, but imagine things as bodies and through our vibrational coexistence, where we appear fragile, unreliable and relational, confronting of a certain form, and therefore inviting of a conversation that does not show me art but shows me myself viewing.

Exhalation: Restless rest

In many ways, this chapter turns around, turns on its head, reverses and approaches from another side, without being oppositional, my earlier suggestions on curatorial volumes, made for example at a 'Study Day for Displaying, Collecting and Preserving Sound Pieces' at Tate Britain in 2017.[19] Then I proposed sonic volumes as providing a different spatial imagination and the possibility to curate a different view, opening new dimensions and providing a connecting logic for the curatorial project.

Now I am working backwards, but to the same point. Thinking this volume as a political, as an aesthetico-political dimensionality, generated

---

[18]Voegelin, *Political Possibility of Sound*, 46.
[19]'Curating Volumes: Hearing Architecture, Light and Words' – Paper given in the context of *On Space and Sound*, Collaborative seminar between British Art Network and Contemporary Art Society, at Tate Britain 27 October 2016; to listen: https://www.con temporaryartsociety.org/resources/space-sound-study-day-displaying-collecting-pre serving-sound-pieces/ (accessed 8 June 2022).

from indivisible and formless human and more than human bodies in training. I do this in the hope of gaining a means to unconceal and resist the violence of legislation and curatorial control, which depends on a conventional language and a conventional architecture of walls, ceilings, floors and doors to retain its justification. What I am suggesting is that the voluminous dimensionality of sound, its indivisible relationality, does not only provide a different aesthetic possibility for curation, but that additionally or as a consequence of approaching the curatorial not through spatial organization, as an ordering frame, but through the work and bodies producing a voluminous sphere, the violence of aesthetic practice and of politics is unconcealed, and we are provided an opportunity to approach this violence with care-full possibilities for creative resistance and an entangled imagination.

The creative resistance and entangled imagination enabled by this voluminous sonic dimensionality do not stand in opposition to viewing and a visual sensibility, but question a conventional visuality and seek to see differently – to see the body in its relationality and transformation: as chaos and disorder, coexisting contingently in a vibrational world. In this way, the sonic does not propose an antinomic view, but expands what can be seen and sensed beyond conventional language and normative aesthetic/ political expectations. It lets us enter into a possible world made from invisible connections, rather than individuated works and bodies, that sound as simultaneous and plural rhythms the purposeful inefficiency of a thick expanse: the timespace created by detours and off-track movements that are at times not even audible but attain a sonic sensibility and perform a conceptual audibility through the relationality of their material resonance. Together, flesh and material bodies, the work and the space, produce a hum, that makes a volume of different but simultaneous frequencies that build a space from human and more than human interactions, presenting invisibly a restless view. This restless view does not mirror but diffracts the body not as form but in its building and working out, its dancing and singing, walking and looking at work.

I get to this restless and diffracting view via Brandon LaBelle for whom the acoustic sphere has a 'restlessness' that creates an 'opportunity for relating to what is different from me (even of myself), and therefore, contains a deep potential, for greater solidarity'.[20] This restlessness enables

---

[20]Brandon LaBelle, 'Restless Acoustics, Emergent Publics', in *The Routledge Companion to Sounding Art*, ed. Marcel Cobussen, Vincent Meelberg and Barry Truax (New York: Routledge, 2017), 275–6.

a 'radical sharing', which from LaBelle's writing I come to understand as a sharing that works from difference and distance, rather than from a given or assumed proximity and similarity, and that values this difference as part of the shared rather than as an obstacle to its communality. It is from the space between things and humans as things experienced not as a gap but as a connecting sphere that the sonic creates the volume of an always plural *being with*. And it is from distance and difference rather than from an assumed, cultural, political, social or ideological nearness that the sonic generates the collective and proximity. Thus, it is within restlessness, heard as 'the spell of the auditory' that my subjectivity is produced as a sonic subjectivity, that is not only me but that is me with the other in a sonic 'rebound':[21] that is a continual process of sounding and resounding between, creating a diffractive echo that does not call back the same but sounds our mobile difference and distribution. Therefore, I am not present as an individuated, singular self, nor are you. Instead, we are the sound commingling in the in-between and without a certain form, in practice, restless.

This restlessness is not anxious or nervous. It is not a pacing up and down: a sound on hold to burst forth, linear and with an aim. Rather, it is a constant and diffuse vibration that as continuity and inexhaustibility opens a sphere in the visible separation and distance to feel close and response-able. Maybe it is not restless at all but offers a sense of rest and respite that Džuverović and Revell desire and need to take care of themselves. Its constant vibration does not go anywhere, it has no forward pull or desire to progress. Instead, it hovers. It hovers in the space of the work, defining its temporality as expanse, and sounding its connecting sphere, within which the body too is as materiality and as vibration, restless even when still.

When I leave the gallery, the exhibition space, I do not leave a building but a restless sphere that will hover on and welcome the next person to contribute to its vibrations: to cross into its indivisible field; to meet others in a radical sharing that is tacit and sensorial. This sharing is not enabled by words, but through the sonic expanse of material and flesh bodies lingering with works as in a world of connections beyond conventional language. These connections are not necessarily benign. The hum of the artworld that tunes us into the hum of the world is not without disagreement and conflict. But it is caring in the sense that it enables us to think tensions and frictions through connecting and contingent nearness, rather than as others at a distance, or in pre-existing and assumed proximities.

---

[21]Ibid.

Equally, the confrontations of a 'radically sharing' curatorial project are not necessarily benign. But instead of instrumentalizing our audienceship, and legislating our bodies, its care expresses as connecting and creates complicity. It confronts us with our own part in the work, not through reflection, where we remain individuated, at a distance and mirrored through a singular form, but through diffraction, where according to Karen Barad, we read insights 'through one another for their (our) various entanglements, and by being attentive to what gets excluded as well as what comes to matter'.[22] Thus, diffraction takes care of what comes to mean as legibility and on the line, and what comes to mean on the body and through the encounter, so that we can imagine reality through plural relationships and relationalities.

Barad's diffraction is useful to move away from the reflective lines of mirrored representation, which confer (historical) legitimacy through correspondence but fail to take care of less linear and fuzzy possibilities. Embracing her diffractive logic, I see the complex simultaneity and overlaps of bodies in practice, working out and being entangled: reaching neither conventional language nor an individuated form. Bringing Acker and Barad together on this point and on the body, I do not aim for a diffractive *reading*, however, but for a diffractive *working out* of matter and of bodies as matter, to bring us to a careful and attentive understanding that might well remain speechless but is ethical in how it considers what falls beside the line and how that entangles.

A sonic thinking provides the imagination for such an entangled and diffracted mattering. Listening cannot engage in what remains separate but hears our being together in difference and in reciprocity. It hears a restlessness that is not fast and careless, trying to curate the shiny world of art and politics, but that is hovering and invested in the encounter. It is inefficient in relation to meaning and value, but aware of our *being with*: in a vibrational flow of relationships between human and more than human bodies resisting purpose and the insatiable demand of the (art) world, and practising alternatives.

Consequently, it is in a body beyond language but in care-full and cared for conversation that we come to a new possibility of curation as a *process with*, and, to a new possibility of politics as a politics of human and more than human bodies moving together in slow restlessness.

---

[22]Karen Barad, interviewed in Dolphijn and van der Tuin (*New Materialism: Interviews & Cartographies*, 52–3).

This curatorial *process with* articulates and practises the possibility of taking care-full steps, aesthetically and politically, into the unseen, to connect through its invisibility rather than across what can be seen and what we already know. This might provide a more inclusive approach that can cope with bringing into art and into politics also what we do not know how to look at, how to listen to or how to call: the formless and the unintelligible. To access it not in the assumed neutrality of the public space, or through an assumed language and proximity, but through the particularity of the private, that is not the autonomous space of the artist, but that is the private sphere of the unreliable body that emerges into the shared as a process of negotiation, through dancing, listening, singing and moving, generating a contingent proximity.

Thus, curatorial care as political care and voluminous practice can pluralize what counts as art and in meaning and can expand what gains validity. It breaches the conventions of language and the infrastructure of the curatorial and unperforms them in physical training and confrontation not to reject their practice but by coming to curation as performance. As a curatorial performance of works and texts, through which we negotiate the real with the body, as ears, as eyes and as feet: as sensorial limbs in motion, performing together with more than human limbs, the space of the work as a variable entirety but never a piece. And so, leaning on the porous invisibility of sound and the duration of listening I work toward unconcealing the legislation of the look and the violence of value and judgement, to instead practise the care of confrontation and *being with.*

Such a sonic sensibility provides a way to think beyond the curation of pieces as *Stücke*, organized through the curators' judgement and justification, and to resist the curation of the installation as artistic legislation, to instead include everybody/everything in a care that does not depend on un-caring, but on the simultaneity of a sonic possibility to sound and care for everybody/thing at once. Such a curatorial project does not coerce but confront, to create a contingent proximity at its depth, from where I come to see myself in relation to, and come to participate: to work my body through the material and the material through my failure to see a different body and a different work/world.

In this sense, the curatorial project of care is revealed as a political project not by what it curates but by how it negotiates lines of progress, levels of control, legitimacy and authority, and by the way that it brings works and audiences into confrontation.

A curatorial project that cares can address precarity and exploitation; query the offerings of bedazzling shininess and the relentless demand for speed; question the financial *über-purposelessness* of the (art) world; and take account of gender, race and class differences and inequalities. It can do so by transforming how we view and listen together, which becomes a model for how we live together, manifesting the indivisibility of art and politics. It can uncurate knowledge and validity, by putting work beside itself, beside its conventional representation and description, placing it in the thickness of a voluminous dimension, and demanding we take part in its inefficiency: to listen, sing and move together in a slow restlessness; to enter the process of production on detours and on a fuzzy path, rather than viewing the work/world on a straight line.

Performance score

Listen across to uncurate knowledge

A dark floor
A selection of white and coloured street chalks
To one side a record player
To the other side a digital playback device
In-between an empty space
Yourself in dark clothing[1]

Stand at the front of the stage

Take one breath

Introduce yourself

Go to the back of the stage

Take two breaths

Make a straight white chalk line reaching from the very back to the very front of the stage

---

[1] This chapter started as a performance score, written for a curatorial performance at 'être à l'écoute' a symposium on sound at EDHEA (école de design et haute école d'art du Valais) Sierre, Switzerland, that took place on 1 and 2 October 2021. I wrote a score in preparation for the event. I revisited it post-performance, to add and adjust, and to render it at once a documentation and a new score that is an invitation for you to reperform, in order to participate in its proposition and deviate as well as augment its ideas from your own movements, voice and song. All images are taken from this performance video: https://www.youtube.com/watch?v=-0G8xBrWlT0&t=1439s, with permission from EDHEA.

FIGURE 1 Still from curatorial performance 'Uncurating Sound', performed by the author at EDHEA (École de design et haute école d'art du Valais, Suisse) symposium *Être à l'écoute*, 2021 (https://www.youtube.com/watch?v=-0G8 xBrWlT0&t=9s).

Source: Courtesy EDHEA.

Stand next to the line and take three slow breaths.

Read while trying to look at your audience

The title of this performance – Listen across to uncurate knowledge – brings together two ideas that are at the core of my work and research at this present moment.

The first is the notion of knowledge as a matter of curating, whereby curating is understood and practised as organizing, ordering and thus of controlling what and how we can know: determining what carries value; establishing hegemonies and singular knowledge paths; and creating lines made from evidence and reference. This idea is practised in a listening across ordered, disciplinary, cultural, gendered, class, racial and national boundaries that disorders this knowledge and its curatorial frame: to challenge its separations; to question the logic of its exclusions; and to pluralize its paths.

Contemplating these two entangled concerns with you today I want to stress the connection between knowledge and curation. To query the self-evidence and apparent neutrality of how knowledge is displayed and legitimized, and from there to rethink curating through 'uncurating', as scrutinizing and undoing historical and economic lines of thought. Whereby the 'un' does not express a rejection. It does not articulate 'not curating' as in not making accessible and thinkable what we see and hear, but invites to consider the curatorial as providing access to and pluralizing what can be thought, and in a different way.

Thus, uncurating does not not curate, but follows the double negative into an affirmation of curation as an untethering of the curatorial from the strictures of chronology and the expectations of a canonical frame. In other words, it entails an untying of the curatorial and of knowledge from the expectation of evidence and reference tied to singular and approved anchor points, found in history and determining present taxonomies, which confirm semantic lines into the future from what is already there. Instead, uncurating troubles the line and tends to everything else: to what is there but we cannot or do not want to see and hear; the other variants whose legitimacy and interpretation do not lie on a line but materialize contingently, unrecognizably and unnamed in the encounter.

And so uncurating tunes in to the term's root in care, *curare*, the medieval church curate, and his caring for artefacts and souls, to practise a more expansive 'un' and reorganization that includes care for the invisible, the unrecognizable, what is beside the line and troubles its stability.

To practise these ideas today, I will perform through sound making and listening, drawing and moving, a *being with*: to hear myself with everything else, with you, with other human and more than human bodies; and to perform a mattering *with*, which I understand to be the condition of uncurating, as the condition of a dynamic in-between that generates the disorder of knowledge's proper form.

This condition of mattering *with* makes curation performative, rendering it an always live process of human and more than human matter mattering together. Its knowledge consequently too is performative: unstable, unreliable and open; a matter of how we matter with the seen and heard contingently, felt and local. Uncuration as such a relational performance, akin to Barad's 'agential-realism', does not organize and mediate given things, neither through language nor through other infrastructures/apparatuses of meaning and exhibition. There is no separate agent or authority of doing;

instead, matter itself becomes practice.[2] Therefore, human and more than human matter emerge concurrently through a relational becoming that binds together material and discursive practices. The knowledge we gain from such an entangled practice is then not about the curated, as a separate entity, but about our relational constituting of 'the exhibition': of work, of theory, of architecture, of finance, of human and more than human matter. Together.

As such a relational performance practice, curation becomes a discursive knowledge practice that is as Michel Foucault's discursive practice not invested in knowledge as 'connaissance', as (re)cognition of a pre-existing thing or status, but generates 'savoir', the knowing of the emergence of what something is and how it can be known.[3] Therefore, this knowledge does not determine what is shown or what is seen, 'this' or 'that', and it is not about human agency and ability to show or to see. Instead, it is how we emerge with each other, between what is shown and what is seen. How we become visible. And it entails responsibility to this process: the accountability to how being seen and seeing meet each other at vision's depth, where I cannot see myself looking, but come to understand vision's artifice and its reduction to things and bodies, and where I can take responsibility of how matter emerges in the invisible in-between, which as a sphere of sound, even if inaudible or unheard, confirms how matter mattering is indivisible, in that it *is* connecting rather than a theoretical apart.[4]

Such a focus on the relationality of mattering, as a local and tacit knowing from the indivisibility of things, is made accessible, as in thinkable, through sound. The sonic shows us the knowledge of human and more than human bodies from their invisible connecting, from how we sound together. It disrupts and rejects the distance of objectivity, relied upon in conventional knowledge frames. Instead, it insists on proximity and entanglements as the only condition to know the flesh and material body from. Therefore,

---

[2]In her text 'Posthumanist Performativity: Toward an Understanding of How Matter Comes to Matter', Barad, referring to the physicist Niels Bohr, outlines her notion of agential realism as follows: 'in an agential realist account, matter does not refer to a fixed substance; rather, matter is substance in its intra-active becoming – not a thing, but a doing, a congealing of agency' (Karen Barad, 'Posthumanist Performativity: Towards an Understanding of How Matter Comes to Matter', *Signs: Journal of Women in Culture and Society* 28, no. 3, *Gender and Science: New Issues* (Spring 2003): 822). This congealing of agency in doing usefully describes the congealing of doing of uncurating.
[3]Michel Foucault, *The Archeology of Knowledge*, trans. A. M. Sheridan Smith (New York: Phanteon Books, 1972), 181–3.
[4]This notion of depth is developed from Merleau-Ponty's articulation of the back and behind what cannot be seen but what we deduct or synthesis, as articulated in *Visible and the Invisible*, 220.

knowledge *of* is always already knowledge *with*, and its reciprocity ties me into the responsibility of this *with*: to be 'accountable for the role "we" play in the intertwined practices of knowing and becoming'.[5]

This knowledge *with*, questions the singularity of knowledge as well as its normative theorization and structures of display. Conventional knowledge is organized and legitimized along patriarchal lines of reference, assuming the possibility and necessity of distance, between matter as things, as well as between theory and practice. From there it claims legitimacy and universality for a truth that matters wherever you are, within or without its entanglements, and from whatever distance you hear its proximities.

By contrast, the local and the relational disrupt and challenge universal lines of evidence and reference. Thereby, they disrupt the ideologies and histories that are hidden in these lines. Listening and sound making, as always local and relational activities, have the capacity to disorder a visual, taxonomized and singular knowledge. And with that, they have the capacity to reveal through disorder and disruption the ideologies, power plays, investments and interests – political, economic, social and so on – that motivate and enable these organizations and ultimately normalize and perpetuate their interest and point of view, which pretend a universal view that we struggle to correspond to if we are off the line.

The defence of this line is pernicious. It pretends to be unaware of the exclusions made to keep the line and keep it straight, and it feigns ignorance of the political ideologies hidden in its linearity. In this way, the line is kept invisible, naturalized, a vanishing point that controls what can be seen, what can be said, without speaking. This ensures a mute universality that protects its hegemony and generates epistemic violence[6]: the violence of a

---

[5]Barad, 'Posthumanist Performativity', 812.
[6]Epistemic violence is the violence of colonial projects and a Western modernist world view, which is entirely local but postures as universal and installs and legitimizes a particular knowledge framework while subjugating other knowledge possibilities:

> I believe that by subjugated knowledges one should understand something else, something which in a sense is altogether different, namely, a whole set of knowledges that have been disqualified as inadequate to their task or insufficiently elaborated: naive knowledges, located low down on the hierarchy, beneath the required level of cognition or scientificity. I also believe that it is through the re-emergence of these low-ranking knowledges, these unqualified, even directly disqualified knowledges (such as that of the psychiatric patient, of the ill person, of the nurse, of the doctor – parallel and marginal as they are to the knowledge of medicine – that of the delinquent etc.), and which involve what I would call a popular knowledge (*le savoir des gens*) though it is far from being a general commonsense knowledge, but is on the contrary a particular,

knowledge that through its self-evidently universal objectivity oppresses all other possibilities, calling them impossible.

How can you disrupt a line that does not exist, that has been naturalized into invisibility? How can you disrupt a line with a voice that the very line you seek to disrupt has made unimportant, trivial or inaudible? How can you claim legitimacy on another path when only one is possible and that possibility denies the existence of any other?

Sound, when it is not musically orientated, or semantically structured, does not speak in lines or through reference, but follows a relational logic as the logic of a dynamic and disorderly in-between. It is not 'this' or 'that', 'me' or 'you', but everything together, entangled, interwoven, codependent. It does not make maps, lexica or taxonomies, but volumes, generated in the performance of our in-between and *being with* – from the invisible and from how we share in the indivisibility of time and space.

Sound does not make a room with walls, windows, floors and ceilings but creates a voluminous dimensionality, generated from how everything sounds in relation to everything else, without individuation. Thus, we become auditorily aware of our inter-being and as a *being with* of listening and sound making: co-generated from our in-between, where neither of us is but where our sounds meet each other and that of others and of other things, to create an indivisible expanse made from the invisible friction between flesh and material bodies standing at a distance but sounding up close.

In sound we are not reflected but practice diffraction, the bending of light through our simultaneous difference. Thus, we perform the physical

---

local, regional knowledge, a differential knowledge incapable of unanimity and which owes its force only to the harshness with which it is opposed by everything surrounding it – that it is through the re-appearance of this knowledge, of these local popular knowledges, these disqualified knowledges, that criticism performs its work. (Michel Foucault, *Power/Knowledge, Selected Interviews and Other Writing*, ed. Colin Gordon (New York: Phanteon Books, 1980), 82).

Epistemic violence, that is, violence exerted against or through knowledge, is probably one of the key elements in any process of domination. It is not only through the construction of exploitative economic links or the control of the politico-military apparatuses that domination is accomplished, but also and, I would argue, most importantly through the construction of epistemic frameworks that legitimise and enshrine those practices of domination (Enrique Galván-Alvarez, 'Epistemic Violence and Retaliation: The Issue of Knowledges in 'Mother India'', *Atlantis* 32, no. 2 (December 2010): 11–26, 12).

optics of Karen Barad:[7] producing vibrational patterns from our overlaps and tracing invisibly all the ways we intra-act. In those intra-actions, we are constituted together as a *being with* and in proximity however far apart.

This condition of a close up *being with* has become most apparent during the pandemic. Our viral impact on each other emphasizes our overlaps and interdependencies, as well as our asymmetries. We breathe the same air. We breathe the same virus. Thus, we come to sense closeness as critical reality: as a means to know from the in-between and appreciate also where underlying economic, social, geographical, health and other conditions determine our difference.[8]

The pandemic suspends the idea of a critical distance understood as creating objective knowledge and confirming individuation. Instead, it strengthens the experience of a porous and leaky subjectivity as well as of leaky and porous more than human matter and the idea of closeness as criticality, demanding responsibility and care.[9] Since, as I was cleaning groceries of any viral residue and spoke to loved ones only via Zoom and Skype, the sense of self and sovereignty was recomposed as a codependent reciprocity that is vibrational and reflected diffractively in each other and other things, rather than as correspondence and in one mirror. Our focus was on how we experienced this locked down situation, in which differences did not reflect as a matter of separation and individuation, but as continuation and shared possibility. And where thus asymmetries became accessible and thinkable and therefore valid and valuable to the way we know the world/the work.

---

[7] Karen Barad, interview (Dolphijn and van der Tuin, *New Materialism*, 49*ff.*).

[8] Despite sharing the same air, we did not all suffer the same health, financial, social or physical consequences of the pandemic. The impact of the virus was/is so very different, depending on age, income, ethnicity, where you live, underlying health conditions, access to health care and so on, people fared better or worse. But there is also unpredictability and uncontrollability to these categories of protection. They are not rigid or certain. We are all porous, we are all connected, we are entangled: we are *beings with*, with other human and more than human beings and things, breathing the same air. The suggestion is that the closeness and interdependency that becomes thinkable through the virus does not mask asymmetries, or assume their non-existence, but rather that it makes socio-political inequalities more thinkable by bringing them into proximity and thus into possibility: provisionally at least creating a critical empathy and care.

[9] The notion of the feminine body as leaky and porous is influenced by Elizabeth Grosz's idea that 'the female body has been constructed not only as a lack or absence but with more complexity, as a leaking, uncontrollable, seeping liquid; as formless flow; as viscosity, entrapping, secreting' and as lacking self-containment (*Volatile Bodies: Towards a Corporeal Feminism* (Bloomington, IN: Indiana University Press, 1994), 203).

Listening performs this 'pandemic' intra-action. It is being entwined in the world as a volume of shared breath. It is being part of this volume, being complicit and acting from this complicity, since as we listen, we listen from our ears to our hands and feet and move from listening to doing and walking, as an extended practice of what we hear as what we are with. In this way, a listening entanglement is not passive and with an end, to hear in order to understand, but continued in what we do, how we act in a world as sonic beings, as interbeings – enacting a being in listening – performing entanglements and proximities rather than looking to disentangle and to establish distance that might legitimate a knowledge beyond the volume, on a straighter line, but that will miss everything else.

The sense of this entangled and intersubjective volume is not found in the taxonomical, essentially Kantian and modernist system of knowledge that since Enlightenment increasingly favours 'mechanical objectivity'[10] over sensorial sense and that produces a cultural objectivity that eschews the body, ears, hands, mouth and feet, as unreliable and untrustworthy, and that aims for metrics and measurements understood as universalizing, dispassionate, unrelated to a subject position: installing distance as ultimate criterion of legitimacy and truth.

Distance is a criterion that is impossible for sound to achieve.

Instead, sound engages us close up, on the skin and through the body. It reads objectivity, with Barad, as responsibility and response-ability, where knowledge is found on the body and in a contingent exchange with other flesh and material bodies in their process together: touching and being touched even at a distance.

The inability of sound to observe objective distance demands an ethics of response and reciprocity and configures criticism as a practice of entanglements: to engage in how things are together, entwined and codependent in their formation and in their locale. To evaluate and know not through exclusions, which enable measurability and fact, but through effect and affect, which eschew dates and data in favour of a sensorial and reciprocal sense. Thus, it is from the invisible in-between and through sound's relational logic that we can know not only what something/somebody is and means by themselves, but come to know through what effects human and more than human bodies have on each other.

However, even unconsciously and as a cultural determination, Enlightenment and Modernity haunt us with their aim for objectivity, and

---

[10]The concept of 'mechanical objectivity' or 'noninterventionist objectivity' according to Lorraine Daston and Peter Galison describes an objectivity that aimes at combating the unreliability of subjectivity through an expectation of self-restraint and the disavowal of the scientist's own senses. (*Objectivity*, Brooklyn: Zone Books, 2007, 198).

determine our faith in lexica, taxonomies, dates and data, which legitimate the real by opening gaps between things and their articulation, offering a dispassionate view and pretending the possibility of distance: to be neutral, non-orientated, indifferent to our own position and subjectivity or the context of our thoughts and actions. Objective idealism understands the body as fallible and thus as standing in the way of knowing the world in its calculable truth and reality. Objective distance pays no heed to what way we look, as in what way our vision is trained, what sounds we hear, what paths we travel.

This haunting of the objective generates a scientism in philosophy and in art, that pretends the Western notion of absolute truth[11] that is the understanding of science as objective, non-humanistic, rational, universal and empirical, not connected to cultural values, or location, gender or racial specificity and so on.[12]

To preserve this truth, the standard-bearers of knowledge exclude sonic proximity, the embrace that sound calls us into: its relationality and closeness that defies conventional notions of objective distance and legitimacy, and that instead carries the rigour of a sensorial sense, whose subjective nature makes it appear disorderly, unstandardized and non-standardizable,

---

[11]According to Eric Voegelin, scientism, which he identifies as a conviction born from mathematics in the second half of the sixteenth century, and carrying not only scientific, but also political and social significance,

> began in a fascination with the new science to the point of underrating and neglecting the concern for experiences of the spirit; they developed into the assumption that the new science could create a world view that would substitute for the religious order of the soul; and they culminated, in the nineteenth century, in the dictatorial prohibition, on the part of scientistic thinkers, against asking questions of a metaphysics.

In other words, in a post–Second World War context and as a political philosopher, he outlines and critiques scientism as the dominance of an objective, mathematical, scientific thinking and its oppression of philosophical and therefore ethical enquiries into the production of reality.

He concludes, 'The damage of scientism is done … as a consequence of the interlocking of science and social power, the political tentacles of scientistic civilization reach into every nook and corner of an industrialized society, and with increasing effectiveness they stretch over the whole globe.' And so he articulates the colonial thinking of scientific objectivity as a social power that broaches no other approach to how reality is thought, and that thus subjugates other knowledges and globalizes a Western view (Eric Voegelin, 'The Origins of Scientism', *Social Research* 15, no. 4 (December 1948): 462–94, 462).

[12]Glen Aikenhead, 'Whose Scientific Knowledge? The Colonizer and the Colonized', in *Science Education as/for Sociopolitical Action*, ed. W. M. Roth and J. Desautels (New York: Peter Lang International, Academic Publishers, 2002), 151–66, 151.

unreliable and even vague. Through these attributes, sound is associated with the feminine and the other. It is derided as unscholarly, irrelevant, not a proper knowledge paradigm, when in truth, its awkward refusal to toe the line is the rigour of its criticality, and in that it is neither unreliable nor vague. It is certain in its troubling disorder that is threatening to the foundation of Western knowledge, to the taxonomical formation of its thinking and the certainty of its lines. Sound is the decolonial, feminine, minoritarian, the marginal. It materializes the unrecognizable and what cannot be read; what holds less value and can be ignored because it is not visible, not linear, not individuated and thus not taxonomizable.

In response, I want to relish sound's disorder not as a stance against communication and truth but in acknowledgement that the price we pay for order lies in its exclusions: in what we get rid of to keep the line, what we ignore to keep an order and what we reject to stay structured and recognizable. Because, the lines and shapes we build in curation, as an organizing of knowledge and of artefacts, to make them recognizable, accessible, valuable, readable, are ideological and they are colonial: they are informed by money, bodies, land and power, their worth and exploitation.

Tate Modern is a convenient stand-in here to make a point and show a line. Others can no doubt be found in the history of almost every museum and knowledge institution.

The lines of ships from Africa to deliver slaves to the plantation in the Caribbean and the South of North America meet the lines that deliver sugar to Europe, meet the lines that build a canon of what is good art, valuable, important, what carries knowledge and how to organize it. They are lines that make a map of art, sugar and colonial efforts. These are lines of power gained and lives lost and money made that determine the lines of art and of knowledge. They determine whose knowledge and whose aesthetic, and thus whose order, is considered orderly. Who is in charge to take care of this order to curate it, which is a process that always inevitably creates lines.

This is not to say that every curator and every curatorial project is colonialist or to dismiss the project of curation. Instead, it is an invitation to rethink the notion of organization, order, aesthetics, knowledge and so on, which the curatorial project stands for and creates; to be aware of the invisible line which always already organizes our organizing. In order not to simply fatten the line, but to denaturalize its shape and status, and to make visible the pernicious claims of its invisible linearity, in order to transform its chronology into volumes that are expansive but formless; that are plural, disorderly, unrecognizable, loud and noisy, as well as silent; and that show us the logic of the in-between and the indivisible rather than what something means.

FIGURE 2 Still from curatorial performance 'Uncurating Sound', performed by the author at EDHEA (École de design et haute école d'art du Valais, Suisse) symposium *Être à l'écoute*, 2021 (https://www.youtube.com/watch?v=-0G8 xBrWlT0&t=9s).

Source: Courtesy EDHEA.

Because, while not every curatorial project is colonial, the institution of the museum, and its structure of display and organization, its historical provenance and present affirmation, *is* colonial. The curatorial organization of knowledge in lines of evidence and reference is colonial, and it is a cultural colonialism that is invisible, hidden in the line but made visible in the museum's infrastructures, its hierarchies, locations, architecture, in the habitus it instils and demands of its visitors and the values and validities it fosters. However, these traits are not seen in relation to the ideologies and politics of art. They are not what art looks like but are the mechanism that make art visible while themselves remaining invisible.

Sound has the capacity to make them audible.
Sound can disrupt the line.

We listen on the line to the line – architectural, infrastructural, financial, musical, artistic, geographical, semantic and so on – to hear as recognition and confirmation a legitimated present, but remain deaf to anything else. We are therefore unable to move our hands and feet in a different way. However, we can also listen to generate, in reciprocity and as practice, not of the familiar and in recognition but as disruption and to trouble what draws the line. To hear from the in-between the invisible: that which is not on the line, and is not in the canon, what finds no mention in a historical system of reference and evidence but has to invent itself.

Hélène Cixous and Catherine Clément talk of 'woman', who cannot find herself in history but has to invent herself.

'What is my place if I am a woman? I look for myself throughout the centuries and don't see myself anywhere' … 'Where to stand? Who to be?'[13]

They invite her to give up on the lexical definition and call herself by her own name, in her own story, so she does not have to look for herself in history, where according to Cixous and Clément she cannot be found. Instead of looking for an image that even if found would only represent what she is supposed to be rather than what she is, she has to invent herself, listening, singing and dancing, without fear of definition. In the certainty that the song will let her transform and change, becoming a subject not through the name, the lexicon, the structure of the semiotic and lines of grammar, but through movements of the body with hands and feet, which calls itself and in proximity with all its variant possibilities and all the human and more than human beings it is a *being with*.

Celebrating the possibility to call herself, I do not mean to reduce this exclusion to women but invite everybody to think of how they are organized

---

[13]Cixous and Clément, *Newly Born Woman*, 24.

in the lexicon, orientated by culture and defined in history. To ask and whether they feel represented by that description or want to call themselves by a different name? To gain a space and a body for other possibilities, off the line …?

In this way, 'woman' reads as a stand-in for all who do not find themselves in history, and Cixous and Clément's question offers a place to practise a different position. Use it to write your own lines, and think how you live your identification. To rethink its source and norms by living in the entanglement of a sonic volume rather than on a visual map.

And once you hear that dimension, you can start to move your hands and feet in a different way and along plural lines and lines disrupted through the sound of their possibility.

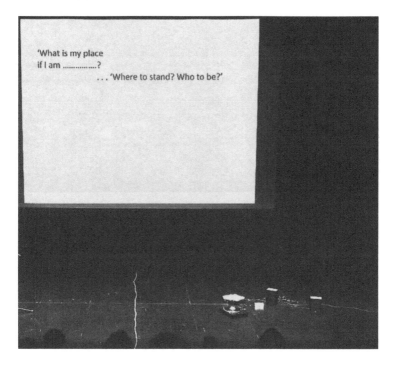

'What is my place
if I am ……………?
……. 'Where to stand? Who to be?'

FIGURE 3 Still from curatorial performance 'Uncurating Sound', performed by the author at EDHEA (École de design et haute école d'art du Valais, Suisse) symposium *Être à l'écoute*, 2021 (https://www.youtube.com/watch?v=-0G8 xBrWlT0&t=9s).

Source: Courtesy EDHEA.

FIGURE 4 Still from curatorial performance 'Uncurating Sound', performed by the author at EDHEA (École de design et haute école d'art du Valais, Suisse) symposium *Être à l'écoute*, 2021 (https://www.youtube.com/watch?v=-0G8 xBrWIT0&t=9s).

Source: Courtesy EDHEA.

It is from our own historical lines and how we want to live them, how we want to orientate ourselves, that we can come to understand the construction of the universal, the objective and apparently singularly normal, and that we can come to comprehend our complicity in and experience of epistemic and identitarian violence: to be called rather than calling yourself in an incontrovertible system that mistakes its local contingency for universality. And it is from the relational logic of sound as a feminist and decolonial logic of relational volumes that we can practise knowledge and subjectivity as the unreliable specificity of ears and hands and feet that query the line and queer the line.[14]

In sound's close-up disorder and unrecognizability, we can reconsider the line's direction, homogeneity and orderliness. We can query its provenance and aims, and blur its timeline and spaceline, creating the fuzzy geography of a plural knowledge and plural *beings with*.

Start to play Kate Carr's piece *Hawkes End – River Sowe Junction – A Sonic Transect of the Sometimes Absent River Sherbourne* (2021).

Take four breaths

Walk across the line and switch on the record player, playing Ellen Fullman's *In the Sea* (1987) without turning up the sound.

Take the chalks and get to work for 10 minutes troubling the straight chalk line drawn earlier with alternative lines and drawings.

Switch Carr's track off, but keep Fullman's record turning without sound.

---

[14]Such a querying and queering of the line of bodies and of knowledge, has been performed for example by Chanda Prescod-Weinstein's *The Disordered Cosmos: A Journey into Dark Matter, Spacetime, and Dreams Deferred*, 2021, and by Jennifer Lynn Stoever in her book *the Sonic Color Line*, 2016, or by Gregory Barz and Michael Cheng, in *Queering the Field*, published in 2019, and earlier already by Siobhan B. Somerville in her book *Queering the Color Line*, which through analysis of cultural artefacts and movements shows the intersections of gender, race and sexuality and the interrelated investments to draw such lines in order to reinforce terminology and definitions.

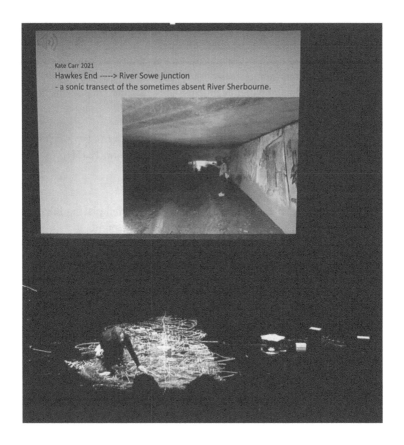

FIGURE 5 Still from curatorial performance 'Uncurating Sound', performed by the author at EDHEA (École de design et haute école d'art du Valais, Suisse) symposium *Être à l'écoute*, 2021 (https://www.youtube.com/watch?v=-0G8 xBrWIT0&t=9s).

Source: Courtesy EDHEA.

The record player did not play a sound, it only turned and brought us its own mechanical crackle, created from a needle touching a line that is not straight, that does not move on linearly but goes round and round, re-meeting and moving on in circles; and that does not move outwards and onwards in a progressive sense, but comes from the outside to the middle, ever smaller, tighter, creating a point rather than a line.

Instead of Fullman's record, which is turning still on mute, we heard Carr's field recording composition of the river Sherbourne, produced for the Coventry Biennale, UK, in 2021. The river Sherbourne is a river that sometimes is not there, that disappears underground and yet flows on, to surface again. It has been shaped by humans through urban planning, into this undulating, appearing and disappearing existence that interrupts its open flow, to build a town and enable transport. Design ideas and commercial interests have organized its structure and curated its paths to serve a human purpose. Inversely, this has also organized and curated how people live and move in that town. Where they can go with more ease because the river is not there, and what they cannot reach and hear because the river has been buried underground.

Carr is an artist, composer and researcher interested in transects. These are lines that allow geographers, biologists and anthropologists, among others, to draw a line and to research along its run rather than in an open field. Thus, it provides a measure and comparability. By coining the term 'sonic transect' and working with sound's invisible diffusion, Carr at once uses and disrupts this measure: bringing sound as a legitimate focus of research to the lines of the aforementioned disciplines, while also querying the methodology and limits of their visual approach that practises quantification but loses the ephemeral. In this way, her work shows how sound expands the line, giving it time and volume; and how this ephemeral expansion troubles its measure by sounding the limits and exclusions it must practise to stay a line. Carr's work makes a fuzzy geography that makes audible what needs to be ignored, overlooked and wilfully excluded to make and sustain a line; and it agitates against those exclusions to bring us the continuity of a river that is sometimes absent and off the line.

To understand and discuss the criticality of this absence not simply as an aesthetic play of negatives, I look at the absence that defined sculpture in the 1960s and 1970s. Through this connection, I query my own modernist haunting, and think the disappearing of the river Sherbourne through how it meets and rejects the negative of an anthropocentric and colonial world view. In particular, I think its absence in relation to negativity, which Rosalind Krauss writes about in her essay 'Sculpture in the Expanded Field' from 1979. In this way, I meet from the sonic another expanded field and search for its edge and boundary and its claim to criticality, to investigate its material relations and to query its possibilities vis-à-vis those of sound.

One of the works discussed by Krauss is Robert Morris's work *Untitled (Mirrored Cubes)* from 1965. This is an installation of a number of cubes made out of mirrors positioned in a particular site, the museum, or in the case of the installation at Green Gallery, outside, on green grass. Their reflection does not show a cube but reflects the environment and the

FIGURE 6 Still from curatorial performance 'Uncurating Sound', performed by the author at EDHEA (École de design et haute école d'art du Valais, Suisse) symposium *Être à l'écoute*, 2021 (https://www.youtube.com/watch?v=-0G8 xBrWlT0&t=9s).

Source: Courtesy EDHEA.

viewer in that environment, disguising the sculpture in its own materiality and site of installation. According to Krauss, the work performs everything that is not it, that is not sculpture, that does not perform its historical category and material expectation. What we see, or rather fail to see, are mirrors that reflect the green grass and which through this reflection remain invisible as sculptural objects. Morris's sculpture is so Krauss, the combination of not-architecture and not-landscape, or what she terms 'the combination of exclusions'.[15] Two exclusions that to her represent the

---

[15]Rosalind Krauss, 'Sculpture in the Expanded Field', *October* 8, Spring (1979): 36.

limit of modernist sculpture, which has entered 'the full condition of its inverse logic and had become pure negativity'.[16] Sculpture has become its own outside and creates an expanded field where the category of sculpture subsumes architecture and landscape – two terms which were so far understood as antithetical to its practice – into its fold, making sculpture the combination of both.

Her reading of Morris's work articulates an ontological absence: a disappearance of category that, however, imminently resurfaces and is reinstated through a modernist thinking and visuality that believes in objectivity and thus ultimately in presence. The visual sculpture, the mirrored cubes, does not disappear but makes itself present through its subsuming of landscape and architecture, which disappear into its terms. The sculptural absence is dialectical, as its theology is hyper-invisible: its truth and belief system so omnipresent that it does not need to be seen.

Therefore, while the mirror surfaces of the cubes disguise the sculpture in the reflection of green grass, the work does not disappear. Instead, it is the absence of landscape and architecture, as experiential spaces, that get sucked into the mirror's reflection. The cubes create a blackhole that swallows the environment to keep its own form. While a concurrent sculptural discourse makes space for and confirms the work's hyper-invisibility, by writing the subjugation of the environment into the artistic and curatorial order. The negative in Morris's work makes everything part of the sculptural, as an expanded field, and thereby brings everything into the order of the museum, the context of art.

The Ultimate Tidy Up.

Nothing remains uncontrollable, disorderly: nature is landscape, space is architecture, and both are sucked in and organized as art.

The work performs a hoovering outdoors, defining the postmodern madness and conviction that it is still possible to find a homogeneous order in the face of gender, racial, class and other heterogeneity, and that the human as universal and unified category remains intact and central despite the damage done through a Western, anthropocentric view. The mirror stands for a high modernist hope that we do not have to abandon the modernist line if we just make it invisible. All we need to do is expand the framework of inclusion and change terminologies.

[16]Ibid.

In this sense, this negative of sculpture is comparable also to John Cage's *4′33″*. His silence performed in the concert hall, with a piano, and a performer, for 4 minutes and 33 seconds does not trouble the category of music but categorizes silence. Through his work, performing the absence of music, music does not disappear as an aesthetic knowledge category. Instead, Cage's *4′33″* makes silence a matter of musicology, a 'disciplined' and organized sound. Thus, silence as music's negative becomes sucked into musicological control. Its ambiguity and uncontrollability organized within a musical frame.

Cage's silence is the sound of everything in the concert hall, which through his work becomes recognizable and ordered in musical terms: everything is music now, and this music remains a Western, singular, hegemonic concept. Once ordered, silence loses its blurring relational potential and cannot create

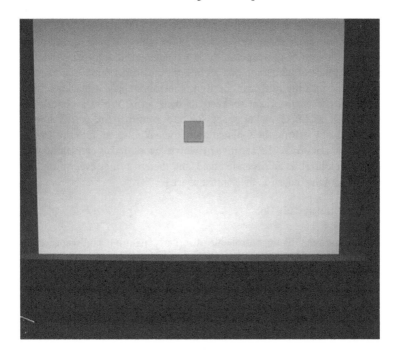

FIGURE 7 Still from curatorial performance 'Uncurating Sound', performed by the author at EDHEA (École de design et haute école d'art du Valais, Suisse) symposium *Être à l'écoute*, 2021 (https://www.youtube.com/watch?v=-0G8 xBrWIT0&t=9s).

Source: Courtesy EDHEA.

the criticality of proximity and fuzziness; and music becomes unperturbed by the possibility of such silence as it has performed its material actuality as category. Thus, silence in the concert hall, like reflected grass, becomes a small square, the negative: silence or landscape/architecture distilled into representability; reduced to the discipline rather than disrupting it.[17]

By contrast, sound, beyond music as aesthetic category, does not order but disorders and disappears the work into the possibility of becoming anything and combining with other possibilities and disciplines. It performs the possibility of becoming a *being with* rather than a being music, being art. And from here, it can start to transform aesthetic and intellectual as well as affective knowledge possibilities, expanding what we know and what we do not yet know, what will become accessible once we work through the proximity of care and responsibility with a knowledge that matters.

Sound questions the modernist belief in an absolute, given presence and truth that haunts Krauss's writing and that haunts all our sense of the real and haunts the curator, the museum and the gallery as agents and locations of order. They are as colonial agents who can keep to the line or can decide to decolonize themselves: to get beside the line, to be able to truly hear the materiality and how human and more than human matter matters disorderly.

In this same sense, and trying to practise this possibility of a non-linear sonic knowledge, I understand that while the river Sherbourne has been made into a line and silenced, it keeps its sound in disappearance and designs an underground world that we cannot see but that has an impact beyond the visible, as a metaphysical imagination that resists the scientism of lines and eschews its negativity. Bricks, walls and modern technology have organized and straightened the river, but its sound bounces into a diffractive plurality of what we cannot see.

Walk across the now plural lines and gestures on the floor.

Switch on the volume of the record player. Let it play for 3 minutes.

Underneath and in the background of all my talking, drawing, walking and breathing, and Kate Carr's river, turned Ellen Fullman's sound of the Long String Instrument. An instrument of variably long and often

---

[17]I hold an appreciation for Cage's Silence, and what it tried to enable: to bring the queer, the odd, the non-musical into the space of music, to trouble its space and convention. This is not a critique of what he intended but a critique of the circularity of aesthetic and disciplinary violence that forever reorders what we start to imagine in disorderly ways.

site-specifically set up steel wires, which she has been developing since the 1980s, and which she would play with rosin-coated hands. Her work *In the Sea*, from 1987, initially recorded on cassette tapes, creates a droning band of tones and vibrations that undulate and fluctuate, while staying continuous. The manual play of long strings creates overtones that respond to and play not only the instrument but the spaces and bodies, human and more than human matter, that entangle in its vibrations. Thus, the work brings forth a fuzzy architecture of lines troubled by fingers and troubling air, vibrating with everything, sounding everything and making accessible the mattering of matter as the condition of being in the world.

Fullman's sonic string is never straight, square and tidy, but vibrates with everything it is made of and everything that is surrounding it: human and more than human matter that are touching it invisibly. Thus, it generates a volume of vibrational entanglements made from what is on the line and from its exclusions, without drawing them into a certain light, but superimposing their possibilities on how we see the world. In this way, it performs our indivisibility and the agential realism of a physical optics that as an auditive or sonic optics makes us sense rather than think our intra-actions as complex interdependencies.

My not playing her sound out loud, only letting it turn silently on the turntable, until this very last moment in my performance talk, did not define an absence as pure negativity. Instead, it performed the condition of our presence. Of how we were in this room together all this time. How we are together as vibrational inter-beings and inter-matter always and everywhere, indivisibly. Because, even inaudibly, sound agitates an invisible vibration of everything with everything else through which and from whose in-between we are *beings with* and come to knowledge as a fuzzy field of possibilities, which includes our own and performs across, on top of, beneath, beside and troubling the line.

Take five breaths

Given the material condition of our existence as invisible and also inaudible vibrations in indivisible entanglements, knowledge and curation as well as the curation of knowledge would find a better, more critical place for its discursive practice in the vibration of Fullman's strings than in reference to a historical and canonical line, to the structure of the semiotic or to lines of grammar.

Practice is a body of evidence and the condition of evidencing. Therefore, to understand at once what is absent and what is present, and to deal with an entangled world, we need to be in conversation with practice so we might understand its voluminous vibrations and not reduce it to a linear history and a theoretical line.

FIGURE 8 Still from curatorial performance 'Uncurating Sound', performed by the author at EDHEA (École de design et haute école d'art du Valais, Suisse) symposium *Être à l'écoute*, 2021 (https://www.youtube.com/watch?v=-0G8 xBrWIT0&t=9s).

Source: Courtesy EDHEA.

Breath 3

With voice and hands

This chapter deliberately performs very personal reflections of two works. One by Marguerite Humeau, called *Weeds*. A spoken word piece performed by the musician Lafawndah, installed in 2021, in the middle of the pandemic, at the Swiss Church in London, a very stark, white, Calvinist Church in the centre of town. This work sounds a voice in recitation of women's names to resurrect them from their exclusion from history and bring them into a present rhythm. The second one is a documentary made by Manon de Boer, *Think about Wood, Think about Metal*, 2011, with and about the artist Robyn Schulkowsky, a percussionist, composer and sound artist whose hands perform different materials to create new thoughts.

The aim is not to theorize the two works, but to come to words that materialize their composition and my experience thereof by practising an exchange. To appreciate the evidence the work supplies as its own knowledge, as a tacit and material knowledge, which we can try to sense not through a detour into theory, but on our body and in conversation: performing 'a contestation of the excessive power granted to language to determine what is real', by using our own voice and hands to conjure plural realities.[1]

This engagement relies on the subjective and sensory position of myself in critique of distance and its construction and provides the possibility to abandon the category of objectivity. It presents a strategy to undo conventional interpretations and their infrastructures of legitimation, to instead reach the material of the work and its knowledge through a

---

[1]Barad, 'Posthumanist Performativity', 801–31, 802.

contingent perception that is attentive and rigorous in its practice and does not rely on theory to come to understand.

In this sense, this chapter responds to the idea of meaning and value gained through measure and measurability, and rejoins the problem of objectivity discussed earlier: identifying at its core a distance, however small, that creates a gap, which language fills, to organize a world where things can be represented and categorized and where subsequently they are understood through that category rather than their contingent materiality and performance. And through this gap that distance creates and from which meaning takes its form by closing it in correspondence, ethics too becomes caught up in representation, as from this meaning that filled the gap and furnished its valuation, ethics tells us how to think and judge in relation to a taxonomical truth rather than lived experience, and so it offers us no means to know how matter does contingently.

This chapter is informed by listening as a process that participates, that does not register distance but performs entanglements, through which contingent subjectivities and plural realities are revealed that are not representational but are a matter of relationality and of experience. It aims to narrate this entangled subjectivity not as an anthropology of the other but as a sonic anthropology of the in-between and of interdependencies; of my listening now as an ethical and response-able hearing of how I and you and more than human bodies are together and with each other. Such a relational listening unsettles singular actualities in favour of plural fictions that are not untrue but reveal the possibilities of the world and of how else we could think it.

This is a decolonial practice that does not seek to decolonize 'the other', the colonized, or to claim a universal decolonial strategy. Instead, informed by Walter Mignolo and Catherine Walsh it understands that while decoloniality has a global aim, it is always necessarily a local endeavour; we can never decolonize someone else.[2] And it recognizes in their advocacy for relationality, 'the pluriversal and interversal paths that disturb the totality from which the universal and the global are most often perceived',[3] an advocacy for a sonic thinking, that can unsettle singular views through sound's plural and connecting logic.

Therefore, this chapter thinks sound and listening as part of the decolonial practices described by Mignolo and Walsh. It trusts that

---

[2]Walter Mignolo and Catherine Walsh, *On Decoloniality, Concepts, Analytics, Praxis* (London: Duke University Press, 2018), 2, 11.
[3]Ibid., 2.

'relational ways of hearing the world' can deliver opportunities to trouble Western ontologies and self-certainties, to create awareness of privilege and biases and to generate a shift in sensibility towards a position aware and critical of its dominance.[4] Thus, this chapter performs an attempt at an 'auto-decolonization' through listening: to become an 'I' in entanglements; aware of my complicity in the violence of a singular truth and hopeful of developing the ability to attain plural perspectives and to reject the colonial frame of privilege and power, and the claims of its universality.

This practice understands distance, the seeming neutrality of objectivity, to be the basis of a colonial politics since it is through distance that the other becomes the other, and thus governable: available to grasp, name, categorize and use, to colonialize. And it is through distance as the guarantor of unaffected measurability that knowledge pretends to be rational, unbiased and universal, not connected to cultural values, location, gender or racial specificity, and thus oppressive of those very specificities.

The desire for 'mechanical objectivity',[5] burning since Enlightenment in the West, is the precondition of this distance as a modernist and thus as a colonial ideology, enabling labels and valuations that lead to exploitation of flesh and material bodies because the gap between word and meaning enables representation and eschews responsibility and empathy. It lets us grasp, and lets us off the hook. Things become a matter of semantics rather than marks on bodies, and bodies become goods to be had and formed, drawing a straight line from Enlightenment to neoliberalism: from a knowledge ideal that seemed emancipatory to exploitation.

The knowledge of objective distance in its claim to universality is, however useful it might be for modern science, always already colonial and therefore violent and oppressive of other ways to see and think. Ultimately, its benefits remain benefits only if not measured against what else we could know, as that remains oppressed, and thus in a current frame unthinkable and unknowable.

The knowledge of proximity, reached through an entangled listening, can make us think about these exclusions, about what distance stands for,

---

[4]The phrase 'relational ways of hearing the world' is an adaption of Mignolo and Walsh's own phrasing 'relational ways of seeing the world', which they attribute to the feminist decolonial projects of Sylvia Wynter, Audre Lorde and Yuderkys Espinosa, who emphasize the need to see 'the relation between privilege and oppression' (ibid., 17).

[5]The concept and aim of 'mechanical objectivity' is described by Lorraine Daston and Peter Galison in their book *Objectivity* as the scientific requirement to suppress one's own subjectivity and ignore the testimony of one's senses, to ensure a repeatable and reliable scientific process. (Brooklyn: Zone Books, 2007), 198.

ideologically and politically and in terms of scholarship. And it can make us think how we can unperform it – how we can embrace a plural knowledge from the contingency of matter rather than from representation: practising tacit, feminist, local and contingent knowledges that become possible when the demand for objective distance is abandoned and closeness and subjectivity become legitimate and valuable. From this close-up and subjective *being with*, we can practise an ethics of proximity that means taking responsibility for how we are positioned and orientated in the world, and for how we are with human and more than human bodies in a *knowing with* rather than organizing them.

To try this unperformance of distance and embrace plural and material knowledges, I listen to Marguerite Humeau with Lafawndah and Manon de Boer with Robyn Schulkowsky while thinking of an anthropology of proximity that creates in words impressions of materiality, as impressions on my body, that do not mean explicitly but performatively: where we matter relationally and through the traces we leave on each other. Such performative knowing circumvents, through touch and sound, the very fact that our habits of looking and our expectations of seeing cover, as in obstruct, our coexistence. And it makes apparent the involvement of language in this obstruction, as it is language, as theory and grammar, that represents bodies touching but demands distance and distinctness to make its point.

The sonic, by contrast, refuses this distance. It touches my skin. Close up however far. It leaves no gap and thus no opportunity for simple correspondence. It makes me part of what I mean to measure: myself a part of knowledge's materiality, without a representational language to prise open a space for reflection and objectivity, which in any event would be unable to reach the level of the skin.

But how to write without that gap? How to make language sing a song of entanglements and proximity without losing legitimacy and a voice? How to be critical without that notion of critique that distance affords and installs as proper practice?

I am assured and guided in this endeavour by Steven Feld's notion of 'acoustemology',[6] a combination of acoustics and epistemology, generating a knowledge from sounding and listening, as arrived at through his field

---

[6]Steven Feld, 'Acoustemology', in *Keywords in Sound*, ed. David Novak and Matt Sakakeeny (London: Duke University Press, 2015), 12.

work in the Bosavi Rainforest region in Papua New Guinea. Here the trees are too dense to afford a distant view, and orientation has to be found on the body and with other bodies up close: through touch and smell and sound.

This knowledge is grounded in a local practice, a proximous geography without lines but viscous volumes of trees. It does not find meaning through representation and correspondence but senses relationally, from how sounding is a listening *with*. Thus, Feld comes to understand how Bosavi song is not an adaptation or response to, but a participation in the relationality of the forest. It cannot offer a separate (ethno-musical) category that could be investigated through conventional scholarship, away from the lived environment and within pre-existing theory because this would not hear the conversations and connections made by the song but only pull its relational interactions into a linguistic/representational frame, excluding their material, local and contingent knowledge.

After more than fifteen years of embedded research in the region, Feld comes to understand that conventional anthropological methodologies and knowledge paths will not hear the indivisible field but remain focused on separating the trees from song, from bird call, from insect chirping and so on, to theorize their categories.[7] In response, Feld devises acoustemology to 'theorize sound as a way of knowing' and stages 'inquiries into what is knowable and how it becomes known, through sounding and listening'.[8]

Acoustemology is conceptualized and practised as a critique of conventional anthropology for its human-centred approach and its colonial history. Referring to Audre Lorde's text 'The Master's Tools Will Never Dismantle the Master's House' from 1984, he states that other intellectual tools are needed in order not to continue to hear signs and signifiers, songs and birds and insects, but to listen to songs with birds with insects in a relational practice that performs a sonic phenomenology of the forest of which we are part.

In this sense, his practice articulates a post-anthropocentric anthropology, that is a post-humanist anthropology, where being human is a matter of being matter with, and where lines of measurement and responsibility do not run back into historical reference to run forwards into observations, which are thus always already expectation and recognition, but instead practise entanglements and possibilities of what we don't yet

---

[7]'So there were many surprises, and after more than 15 years of them I felt that I had exhausted the conceptual repertoire of an anthropology of sound, particularly those approaches deriving from theoretical linguistic, semiotics, communications and more formal theorizations in symbolic anthropology' (ibid., 16).
[8]Ibid.

know. In this way, sounding and listening make visible and thinkable an indivisible forest that cannot be theorized through categories and correspondence but through experience and being matter with. In such a knowledge methodology, listening is hearing connections from the body as matter with other human and more than human bodies mattering, without prepositions, grammatical or ideological.

Feld designs this post-human anthropology from sonic entanglements with plants, with animals, with human and more than human bodies in a geography without distance where proximity determines a contingent sense. His is an anthropology that understands the impossibility of critical distance, and therefore of objectivity as measurement and legitimacy. Instead, it is in the material encounter that meaning is found and where meaning becomes a relational sense able to negotiate expectations and reject pre-existing categories by focusing on a present entanglement. It is from the promise of this entanglement as a promise of a decolonial listening and sounding that I will listen to *Weeds* and *Think about Wood, Think about Metal*, to hear as knowing a contingent and relational sense and sing its materialization:

> She taught me how songs are the collective and connective flow of individual lives and communal histories.[9]

Inhalation: *Weeds* (2021)

Marie Coliné of Bern, the use of heat for delating uterus during labour, died circa 1640, Margeret Isis, Martha, Atia Denamis Obst, Donna Carriage, by the forest fires earth and sky are bound together, Wrongoa Maori, Augustine, Alison Balfour born in the Orkney Ilse of Scotland, strangled and burnt for witchcraft.[10]

To the rhythm of a gong Lafawndah's voice recites names of women who contributed to the development of medicine but who for the most part have been forgotten, left out of official history, eschewed by lexica and text

---

[9]Steven Feld talking about Ulahi, a guide in the Bosavi rainforest who told him about 'how songs sung in a bird's voice linked the living and dead, present and past, human and avian, ground and treetops, village and forest' (ibid., 18).

[10]This is a maybe imperfect transcription of the names and stories narrated by Lafawndah. I might have misspelt some names and could not check them all online or in an encyclopedia, as some are still not recognised and thus do not exist.

books. The gong gives a pulse to names and words that open a view on alternative stories of many women excluded together/as one. It turns into smaller rhythms and drone like noises, drawing a space of sound in which the names are spoken, a dog barks, and other sounds fall vertically without a ground. This is an ephemeral place in which we are voice to ear with names that in their calling create a sense rather than the details and facts of knowledge and of geography: generating a space without a ground or map, which does not proceed from an origin and does not follow border lines, and remembering a knowing that was ignored due to otherness, perceived insignificance and staged illegitimacy.

The knowledge of science as an objective *wissenschaft*, only admits certain voices and certain bodies. Humeau's work with Lafawndah's voice generate another possibility. They unsettle the logic of distance and exclusions through the recitation of invisible names that as invisible bodies bring a sonic logic to what and how we know. This logic is plural, close up and formless. It overflows the category and challenges its eliminations.

Lafawndah calls 'the excess', that which we cannot capture objectively and reminds us of the discrimination, violence and exclusions through which a singular knowledge and its representational scheme are installed. Her voice overflows a hegemonic sense and sings a sphere off the line. She sounds that which could not be accommodated in its rationale due to the alleged irrationality of the called: of her way of working, caring and healing, and how she was in the world with bodies and herbs and thoughts. In its undulating and continuous expanse made of names and rhythms, this sonic sphere creates another imagination of what we could know and how we could heal if we had not excluded her work of care.

Remaining voice, remaining sound, *Weeds* does not pull the names into an archive or a lexicon but keeps them distributed, incomplete, uncategorized, open to an infinity of present and future additions, generating a boundless identity of named and unnamed healers and medics, nurses and carers then and now. Lafawndah's rhythmic recitation sounds the discrepancy between history and its reality, between language as theory and language as bodily narration, highlighting subjectivity as a valiant source of knowledge without celebrating individuality.

Her voice does not separate, it does not name to categories, but voices to connect, to bring together and make a community of women left out, ignored, shunned and killed. She does not focus on the individual, as in a patriarchal identification and celebration of a singular male author/genius. Her voice does not name a singular woman but calls to perform a community of bodies, herbs and wisdom shared. Combined in rhythm, they create a critical mass that makes a plural and complex voice that defies her exclusion and seeming illegitimacy by becoming form together across a historical time and traversing an impossible geography. Generating a sonic woman's body of wisdom and care that defies individuation and a certain form, but expands and remains formless, powerful, entangled.

Within the reverberant architecture of the Swiss Church, a space with bare white walls, high ceilings and one sheer glass front, this overflow of names becomes an overflow of vocal materiality. The names bleed and open many reverberations. Small echoes becoming patterns of sonic exclamations that do not allow for differentiation but generate a diffuse rhythm that continues one name into another, into a plural body, into a formless form that defies the human shape and singularity. Instead, it becomes a wave and force and agency, an idiosyncratic and plural materialization of 'woman' doing knowledge rather than organizing it.

In this auspicious location of patriarchal theology, history and knowledge, Lafawndah's voice does not position and interpret but materializes. She does not identify but draws out and forms from connections and connectivities a different imagination of a body and of knowledge not bound to rationality and reference but practised in its possibility and even in its impossibility: through what we do not know to imagine because we are always already orientated in an actually real world whose boundaries guarantee rationality by performing exclusions. Thus, her voice, summoning through names a formless form brings a sonic logic to what and how we know. This knowledge is plural, unreliable, relational, defying order in favour of touch and smell and song; defying time through simultaneity; and defying space by performing a voluminous dimensionality that is the shape of everything together and at the same time.

We listen to descriptions of ailments and their healing by feminine, tacit and local remedies and knowledges. We hear sound picturing organs, limbs and bodies and their care, conjured from the darkness of an invisible space. A space generated not architecturally or geographically but through Lafawndah's care: her act of naming, performing a voicing of forgotten names, conjuring them into the present, healing their exclusion, not by lining them into history but by imploding history, its linearity, its certainty of dates and place, and creating the surging disorder of feminism and decoloniality in its reverberations.

Thus, we listen outside the archive, outside its rarefied space of knowledge and authority, which enables interpretation and association but only of what is already in there, what has already been categorized and validated. These names and bodies remain outside, uncalled but for Lafawndah's voice that cares for them in her calling and brings their care into our vicinity and imagination.

The archive is the repository of knowledge. It is the centre of science as objectivity and the cornerstone of the colonial. It is the organization of the world in rational terms and from hegemonic voices, setting standards and standardizing expectations: what can be known and how it can be known, organized and understood. Archives add up to a comprehensive scheme of knowledge: clear, transparent, providing evidence and labels for certainty and reference. Its ideology and drive are based on a body that understands itself as individuated, rational, knowable and known to itself; not a savage, a witch or a sorceress; and not the feminine which embodies them all. The auditory archive as a counter-archive is performative. It has no room, no walls, no shelves or labels. Instead, it is physical and contingent. It confronts me with its voice and entangles me in its rhythm. In this sense, Humeau's work calls names but unperforms the archive because she does not bring them into its organization, into history and its standardized knowledge. Instead, she questions the legitimacy of the archive and of history as bearers of a rational knowledge, tied to the logic of objectivity as distance, measurement and quantification, by performing an ephemeral space of invisible names that show the rationale of hegemonic knowledge to be based on exclusions and ignorance, as well as misogyny and hate.

The rhythm of Lafawndah's voice sounds as undulations of a different body that does not fit into the archive, and whose life is in excess of and overflows the measurable: that is leaky and porous, and thus dangerous because inexhaustible and uncontainable;[11] and it conjures alternative and plural knowledges from diffuse reverberations rather than a singular sense from the order of the semantic, generating bodies of knowledge and imagining language leaking out of sounds.

In this way, the work performs the voice as a tool of resistance – that is a resistance to the exclusions of history and of lexica, of archives and taxonomies that found and evidence objective knowledge at the expense of the tacit, the local, the feminine, the indigenous, the contingent and practical that sound makes thinkable. It foregrounds a different knowledge

---

[11]This interpretation of the body as leaking and porous is informed by Elizabeth Grosz's idea that 'the female body has been constructed not only as a lack or absence but with more complexity, as a leaking, uncontrollable, seeping liquid; as formless flow; as viscosity, entrapping, secreting' and as lacking self-containment (*Volatile Bodies*, 203). And it is inspired by Margrit Shildrick's notion of the female body in 'its putative leakiness, the outflow of the body which breaches the boundaries of the proper' (*Leaky Bodies and Boundaries: Feminism, Postmodernism and (Bio) Ethics* (London: Routledge, 1997), 17). This lack of containment and definition, provokes a 'a deep seated fear of absorption' (Grosz) and a sense of 'unease and even horror' (Shildrick). That is the unease and horror also of sonic knowledge, provoking fear of what it does to lines and disciplines.

that does not rely on language as theory but works through exhalations, exclamations, sounds and song to know the body through touch and breath, through *being with*, entangled in the possibility of knowing from voice and hands.

Some herbs are becoming lost because people are not picking them.[12]

Exhalation: *Think about Wood, Think about Metal (2011)*

Manon de Boer teases such knowledge from Robyn Schulkowsky's hands performing metal and wood, whose sound and mark making stand in contrast to historical narrations and open a different voice. This is a documentary or a filmed portrait of Schulkowsky, recorded mainly in her studio in Umbria, Italy, with some images of Berlin Mainstation and the WDR concert hall in Cologne, Germany, two landmarks that are significant in relation to how those sonic marks we hear are made.

We never see Schulkowsky, but only her hands. Touching and playing with metal and wood, and stroking a bow over the edges of a bowl. Working fingers that speak in rhythms and through the skin, which is a third phrase Schulkowsky mentions, 'think about skin', that seems fundamental to her working but which was left out of the title of de Boer's film.

The windows are open, making the studio permeable and spacious. The fern trees moving in the wind outside contribute to its rhythm and expanse. Their sound at once locates and opens the rooms through which the camera moves for the first part, panning along bare walls, without wallpaper or paint, exposing marks of time and use: cracks, gaps, dents in plaster, dimples and indentations, revealing tracks and traces that are material witness to interactions and events. The moving camera sets a scene while exploring what is there, moving over instruments and everyday objects: bicycle frames, commercial tins, scaffolding parts, chairs and organ pipes, drumsticks and plastic packing. The difference between what is an instrument and what is a tool or an object is dissolved through the soundtrack. Things are either and both, depending on a contingent exchange, and everything can be brought and is brought into reverberation. The objects and the house itself,

---

[12]Text element of Marguerit Humeau's *Weeds*, spoken by Lafawndah.

its environment, her body and hands, are made accessible through their interaction and conversation, their touch even if at a distance, which for the most part remains invisible, off-screen, creates a connected sense of place and time that sounds their possibility.

The camera stills on Schulkowsky's hands tapping and drumming a square metal plate suspended by two strings. She tells us, 'I have a tactile connection and also an aural connection to the possibilities of sound, from objects'[13] and talks about the potential of sound in everything, which she identifies as the motivation and source of her work. Her fingers agitating the metal is not a drumming *of*, in a conventional sense. Instead, it is a drumming *with*, reciprocal, performing a response to the material's sonic potential. She does not control, but is in conversation with: listening and responding, creating potentially an infinite loop that in this context generates the durationality of the filmed. Her fingers sound with metal, with wood, with skin. There is no gap from which either is identified separately. Thus, there is no gap through which either enters into representation. Instead, they eschew language and their own name to perform a different knowledge of each other, close up and intimate, without the gap into which language slides to name and thus to distinguish them. They (per) form together a sound that does not identify a source but materializes their contingent formlessness.

The sense I get from this portrait of Schulkowsky is physical. It is about her body, which I cannot see but sense in her interactions as a *body with: with skin, with wood, with metal*. Together they produce a material knowledge that communicates through sound making as a making of marks on human and more than human bodies, revealing a language of scratches, impressions, cracks and dents that does not speak through identification and differentiation, but is a narrator of interactions and relationships, of matter mattering together. Listening, I hear this language unfolding as material relations, bearing witness to the ephemeral and the in-between: the touching and tapping, whose traces memorize entanglements and legitimate their narrative as a viable knowledge to understand things by.

From within this relational sphere generated by the tapping of skin with metal, Schulkowsky starts to tell us the story of her musical development. Of how she studied in the United States and how she moved to Germany to gain a different education, to get, by her own words, deep, deep into the matter of music. Her voice does not tell as much as tries to remember and convey the influences and narratives that shaped her own life and let

---

[13]Manon de Boer, *Think about Wood, Think about Metal*, 2011, at 13:20 minutes.

her make the marks she does. Her voice becomes part of the material. I often lose the semantic track. Instead, I listen to the voice making marks, through breathing, sounding, articulating a body that remains off-screen, unrepresented, but powerful. The voice as instrument and potential sound object draws her body, her biography, her work, her rhythm and hopes invisibly and probingly rather than in certainty. It connects affectively to her telling of the shell-shocked survivors of the Vietnam war, with whom she went to college in the United States and through whom she appreciates the body as form, damaged and transforming.

By contrast, once she orientates herself within music as language and canon, she speaks about John Cage, Karlheinz Stockhausen, David Tudor and Morton Feldman among others, portraying them instead of herself. In (musical) language, she defers knowledge and authority to masculine positions and articulations. And while she is in conversation and on equal terms with wood and metal and her own skin, she is not in conversation but a narrator of these composers to a degree that disavows her own presence. I am disturbed by this deference. I am disturbed to see her lose herself in reference while her body taps and touches, drums and insists and makes audible a very different body, which might remain mute in relation to language but speaks loud and clear in relation to materiality and sense.

The semantic narration loses track of the trace evidence. It loses the body drumming *with*. I do not mind the odd reference, the kinship frames and networks necessary to make work, to reflect and be a musician as a *being with* and in a community of practitioners. But those require, in order to avoid violence and subordination, a care of self as whole and equivalent materiality, to talk as she drums from her skin. The contrast is striking since while her voice speaks through reference a language on the line, which erases her, the hands provide the knowledge of her work and of her body that makes her appear as vital matter.

I ponder this breach – the potential for self-effacement in conventional language and confident celebration with matter – and come to understand the danger of excluding the knowledge gained from hands in agitation: the tacit, local, affective sense that speaks beside language and conventions and carries a different body, that is a *body with* – in entanglements and reciprocation, responsible to marks made in sound and on the wall. This exclusion is not trivial but detrimental to what we can know of ourselves and of the world, and what is legitimate, and what comes to stand as witness and in evidence of our possibilities. It is at once personal and consequential of private orientations, as well as political, defining what norms and expectations we are governed by.

Is it generational? Is it historical? Or is it still the same today? That even from the margins we seek to orientate and understand our actions through the centre, through what has been identified and holds an image and a name?

Are we incapable to reflect who we are in language without losing ourselves in reference and representation? And what about the insights lost when the hands cannot find articulation off the line?

While through the hands our body comes to matter as in a diffractive narrative that does not correspond to a referent or a pre-position, but makes 'patterns of difference that make a difference', that make the body speak as material and in exchange,[14] in conventional language, we disappear in reference as in a reflection, seeing correspondence and identification, but losing difference and entanglements, and the ability to know how we are together and through one another.

Schulkowsky's marks on skin and wood and metal are patterns that bear witness to the entanglements through which her body speaks in its own particular and ethical engagement with the world. Hearing how her hands perform together and with objects, I sense how they articulate without words that position of her biography which for the most part she leaves out in language, her own. And how consequently the knowledge gained about her life and music is not witnessed in her voice as language but through her hands that speak the ephemeral and the intertwined.

Conventional and theoretical language makes a detour into reference and evidence outside entanglements. They perform an impossible distance and avail themselves of the gap between mirror and body, to come to meaning as semantic, historical and objective sense. While this might confer certainty and measurability, we lose the human and more than human body that is the site of mark making and plural entanglements, which materialize through our difference in agitation.

This is not a critique of Schulkowsky, but of education, of history and conventional normative knowledge making that removes the body to get to accepted names and a straight line. That denies entanglements and the performance of hands and voice as a materialization and diffractive action. And it is a critique also of sound studies that does not want to listen off the line, that does not want to perform acoustemology as a relational and contingent practice, but makes a study *of* sound and aims to label and organize, to bring into representation and into a visual episteme, and a

---

[14]Karen Barad, interview: Dolphijn and Tuin, *New Materialism*, 49.

visual discipline, what remains invisible and indivisible, so it might gain academic and scholarly legitimacy but lose its own materiality and sense.

In response, this is an invitation to know from the invisible with voice and hands what might not include accepted names only, nor definitions and taxonomical descriptions, but comes to know another way and from other human and more than human bodies. A way that might be capable of dealing with the complex, interdependent problems and challenges of today, that might have the capacity and courage to leave the discipline and leave the line to think and work where things are entangled, where knowledge is tacit, complex, interdependent just like the problems it tries to solve. This does not mean to abandon language but to come to language from entanglements so it might have the capacity to materialize diffractively, not in correspondence and without gaps, without separation or reference, but as a dense and indivisible materiality of the voice and hands in conversation. Building a different house of knowledge whose outline and plans we do not survey but in whose fabric we are woven.

sound it ⅠⅠⅠⅠⅠⅠⅠ

listen to an object you think is still
listen until you can hear it move
respond with your voice and hands.

Breath 4

Postnormal

*Das Bedürfnis, auf eine neue Art zu schreiben, folgt wenn
auch mit Abstand, einer neuen Art, in der Welt zu sein. In
Zeitabständen, die sich zu verkürzen scheinen, hört, sieht, riecht,
schmeckt 'man' anders als noch vor kurzem.*[1]

This chapter does not write a conclusion. Instead, it keeps on breathing.[2] It
is, as Christa Wolf put it, a 'Fortgesetzter Versuch', the title of the book from
which I quote above, a continued attempt at transformation that is aware
of the obduracy of history and memory when they are taken as reference
rather than engaged with as marks on human and more than human bodies
that find their form in how we live at a present moment and towards an
unknown future, without trying to make it known in advance: 'Prosa kann
die Grenzen unseres Wissens über uns selbst weiter hinausschieben. Sie
hält Erinnerung an eine Zukunft in uns wach, von der wir uns bei Strafe
unseres Untergangs nicht lossagen dürfen.'[3]

---

[1]'The desire to write in a new way follows, albeit with a delay, a new way of being in
the world. At intervals that seem to shorten, "one" hears, sees, smells, tastes differently
than a short time ago (Christa Wolf, *Fortgesetzter Versuch: Aufsätze Gespräche Essays*
(Leipzig: Reclam, 1982), 7).
[2]Elements of this chapter were presented as part of the Russian Year in Germany, at an
online conference staged between the UDK, University of the Arts Berlin, and HSE,
Art and Design School, Moscow. An event which only these few months later that
I am rewriting my contribution, has become much harder to imagine but much more
important therefore too.
[3]'Prose can push the limits of our knowledge about ourselves beyond ourselves. It keeps
awake memories about a future, which, at risk of our own demise, we cannot renounce'
(Ibid., 41).

Motivated by the urgency to push boundaries of knowledge to avoid our own demise, pitched against the sense that a move away from hegemonic knowledge and power, that is singular and claims objectivity, based on measurement and data, seems impossible, I set out to try more radically, more outrageously and more determinedly even to persuade you of its importance and to formulate a radical attempt. And so I try to make visible the mirage of norms and normativity that build limits around how we know. To illuminate from the depth of sound and the darkness of what we do not know or do not want to know the illusion of what we think we know, so we might know differently.

Norms are seen, when they are seen at all, as constructions: cultural, social, political projects of standardization. This assumes a certain authorship and deliberation, which gives cultural, political and social agency and will too much credit and form. Norms are more perfidious. They have no singular agent that could be identified and thus confronted and defeated. Instead, they are a cross-hatched job of privilege, laziness, habitus, comfort, narrow mindedness, bias and manipulation which we are all complicit in. They are arbitrary, and in this arbitrariness sits neglect and a great potential for violence as well as denial, and the abdication of responsibility.

At the point of writing this, almost exactly two years into the pandemic, we hoped to see an end to it. The notion of an end can invariably be interpreted as a return to normality, to how things were, or as the obliteration of everything. Two options which until at least twelve days before starting to write this chapter, when the invasion of the Ukraine by Putin's Russia started, seemed balanced towards the first. But the event of war changes the course of lives and hopes. The urge to go back becomes a more complicated venture, more fraught with the causes and complicities that got us here, and the consequences of being here now. We are, however far away geographically we might be, individually and collectively intertwined in a complex chain of events, determined more by oversight and a trust in norms and conventions than actual design. Therefore, the desire to get back to a pre-pandemic normality has attained a distinctly political dimension. The complex interconnectedness of a virus shared invisibly by breath has opened us up to other, more complex interdependencies of money, corruption, power and exploitation that breach previously assumed borders and aesthetics of difference, to reveal the fragile collectivity of the world.

Extreme events are a catalyst for a different thinking and talking and sometimes render it impossible to speak at all. Fostering the need to defy the language from before, and triggering the search for another one, a defiant muteness and then new utterances, gesture-words, noises, screams. Realizing that all that is connected to normative language has to go, even if that means tending towards madness and inarticulation. Embracing ruptures and alien voices, and letting the small breath we take before speaking linger in silence to find a different voice and a different way to articulate.

How do you go back to trusted norms and organization when their value has just exposed the perfidy of its comforts?

The desire for norms is born of a lack of imagination of different socio-political possibilities and of defeat. It represents the sentimentality and longing for a white patriarchal system associated falsely with the absence of the virus, and the absence of war in Europe, when it itself is their breeding ground. A double bind and a trickery of violence and of oppression, to call on us to reinstate the order that caused the asymmetries that caused the virus and that caused the war, and that was revealed so starkly under the pretext of a better, a war- and virus-free, world.

In response and as a radical attempt against the condition of a defeatist normativity, against the perceived comfort of snapping back into how it was before, and inspired by the alienation experienced through the pandemic, I hope to imagine an 'afterwards', that as a continued attempt enables a sustainable transformation, because it holds within it the knowledge of its own perfidy and the reality of its consequence.

Such a 'postnormal' is not detached from the norm through a dash, inviting a binary imagination and the possibility for inversion. Instead, it evokes the possibility of a post that is entangled with the norm, and thus reveals its asymmetries and the deceit of its comforts. This post rejects the norms while keeping them visible within our consciousness, so that we do not fall into the deception of their prejudiced familiarity that pretends to be the only thing possible.

Pronouncing 'postnormal' aloud forms one word and meets in one sound, generated from their encounter and inter-being, as neither post nor normal but as how they sound together and what they generate in their complex contradictions and uncertainties. Thus, we can practice a postnormal that understands the perfidy of norms, and that, in its attempt to move beyond, keeps to the memories of a future, that hold the possibility of a different present, because of rather than despite our hopes for different paths. Not as an antinomic move, always already holding the possibility of its own and imminent reversal, but as a continued attempt that understands the complex entanglements between the desire for norms and the violent obduracy of their reality. Performing the conflict and contradiction of alternatives with every articulation.

After two years, life pre-pandemic is sometimes hard to remember. Our ease at *being with* each other, handshakes, touches, hugs and kisses, seem to have taken place not only in the past, but in an entirely different world, with a very different sense of what appears possible and with seeming impossibilities that have become real: politically as well as socially, and in terms of the concepts and conditions that frame existence, human and otherwise. These impossibilities include positive and hopeful imaginations. Agitating towards a new generosity, empathy and a sense of care. But they also present as darker and disturbing realities, where care is a decoy for political and technological violence and suppression, and the confident reassertion of patriarchal and supremacist power structures, in broad daylight, as a norm that apparently takes care and reassures, or hidden under the swell of current anxieties and struggles.

At this point, I need to stress that I do not condemn the need to wear masks, or stay home if ill, to be vaccinated if possible and take tests. I see those not as power grabs but as our civic and ethical responsibility to ourselves and to each other, and particularly to the most vulnerable in our society for whose health we are answerable, and by whose welfare we are ultimately measured and judged. Instead, I mean more insidious abuses of power: the installation of emergency legislation to manage state finance without oversight or competition, giving contracts to friends, bringing in bills that reduce human rights, sacking minority board members of national institutions, changing immigration legislation and so on, all carried out under the mantle of care and concern. Those power grabs that used the pandemic to close the space opened to plurality and inclusivity before, by using the desire for the normal to create a hyper-normal: the norm of a ruling class that had seen its influence decrease and saw an opportunity to regain ground in its own image.

Can we hear these transformations? Can we sound with and against them?

Could listening as a critical social practice of nuance, and as a leaning-in when social distance dictates otherwise, prepare us, if not for now, then for the next pandemic, which will surely arrive, should this one ever end? So that we are equipped to sound the possibilities and impossibilities of care and collectivity in a connected world, rather than obey individuated imaginings of power. Can the postnormal give a frame to understand how our way of life connects to the pandemic, how it causes it and determines its consequences? To see the invisible and complex interdependencies that dictate a visual reality, so that we are equipped to understand and respond to their entanglements rather than view and discuss them as separate events.

And yet the 'post' in itself does not deliver transformation, it only opens a space to pause and think. It generates a gap in time, to breathe and linger, or to slip and lose ground, depending on your need for certainty and continuity, or your desire for transformation. In this sense, the post delivers a break or a breath, to reconsider normativity and the certainty of chronology through a more diffuse temporality that embraces the disorder of anachronistic timespace entanglements that enable impossible connections across time and space.

The idea of 'post' carries the past that gave raise to its 'postness'. We need the meeting between post and norm spoken to hear what is at stake in their encounter, and to use this simultaneity of past and future past to confront a present norm. To hear the paradox out loud and make a more radical attempt to transform into a future possibility that knows the perfidy of norms and that recognizes the body on which the virus becomes viable as the central energy of this change.

The virus, as the condition of the present, brings a new focus on the human and more than human body, on the individual as a witness, as a body of evidence and as material articulation. Where marks and traces tell plural stories without recourse to reference and canonical history. And where flesh and material bodies become a direct part of scholarship and understanding, without a detour into theory.

Inhalation: *Only Half the Picture* (2002–6)

Zanele Muholi is a photographer and visual activist. They document and make an archive of images of members of the LGBTQIA+ community in South Africa without seeking to define or organize. Instead, the images are invested in repairing bodies and injustices by refocusing the gaze into a plural and responsible view. It is a long-standing project. Muholi has been photographing the community since the early 2000s, creating diffuse and parallel lines to the political history of South Africa. Showing the complexity of liberation and the paradox of the end of apartheid by celebrating a still oppressed and segregated group. The photographed are not subjects but participants in a photographic project of resistance and re-imagination. They retain authority over their portraiture by choosing their own place, pose, clothes and the manner of being photographed.

This is a collaborative venture of empowerment to redirect the gaze. It positions not the photographed but the viewer. It repositions me in my own light and preconceptions and makes me see myself not in reflection, not through correspondences or the failure to see any, but through diffraction, as the difference of overlapping waves that make a pattern: 'in contrast to reflecting apparatuses, like mirrors, which produce images – more or less faithful – of objects placed a distance from the mirror, diffraction gratings are instruments that produce patterns that mark differences in the relative characters (i.e. amplitude and phase) of individual waves as they combine.'[4] Viewing the work through Karen Barad's diffraction gratings, I do not see the imaged at a distance from myself, as other. Instead, I recognize the complexity of our difference through our simultaneity as waves. Because, once I take away the idea of a defined, individuated and pre-formed body on which to impose my view, I come to understand the reciprocity of our reflection as a diffraction: as a *Beugung*, as a bending of the line that abandons the possibility of straight correspondence and sees instead the complex patterns we make together. And so I get to see relationally: I get to see like listening (waves) and come to see my own viewing position, at vision's depth, which normally I view from but cannot see, but that now becomes clear as the shape of my norms and the opportunity of my resistance to their comfort.

Creating diffractive patterns that mark differences, through the individual works and bodies, and marks on bodies, as they combine in my expanded listening as a bent view, Muholi's photographs change the way I look, and thus the way I come to see. They make me see from the depth of our interdependencies, from the way we overlap and are entangled. In this way, the photographs stop being portraits *of* and become interactions and conversations, even confrontations. They confront me with the frame of my gaze and the limit of my reflection. And they confront the exhibition space with the history of its own image and its dealings with representation.

Karen Barad quotes Donna Haraway as suggesting that 'diffraction patterns record the history of interaction, interference, reinforcement, difference.'[5] Thus it is not about originals or a singular, linear history. Instead, it is about how things are together, in their plurality and codependence. About how our inter-being makes patterns of difference in which we see each other in each other. Here I do not look at you but with you, to see

[4]Karen Barad, *Meeting the Universe Halfway* (London: Duke University Press, 2007), 80.
[5]Karen Barad, interview (Dolphijn and van der Tuin, *New Materialism*, 51).

myself in interaction and take responsibility for my gaze, knowing the violence of its norms.

I articulate this sensibility through Barad and Haraway's 'science of entanglements', which provides a scientific image to explain the invisible interdependencies and responsibilities that I sense the work call out. They give me a 'physical optics' of waves, as opposed to a 'geometrical optics' of particles. They give me a space rather than lines to think with and allow me to imagine the work through movements, pluralities and interdependencies rather than as correspondences and in representation. Thus, they invite me to appreciate entanglements and responsibility rather than distance.

However, my understanding of the benefits of diffraction does not follow through quantum physics, of which I know nothing, and whose imagination remains visual. Instead, I access that diffractive space of overlapping and simultaneous waves through sound, whose unavoidable simultaneity, plurality and formlessness holds the creative and visionary potential that Barad associates with a diffractive thinking. And so, I practice a sonic optics: a sonic sense to see the work not as a portrait *of*, but as a sounding *with*, not of 'this' or 'that' but this with that, in complex entanglements and overlaps, heard as patterns and through the encounter: through how my gaze does not see but meets the image physically, creating the relational space of my perception by sensing our simultaneity. Thus, I stop to see representation and come to sense materialization: the way that bodies realize themselves not within expectation and representation but as contingent forms that I do not recognize but have to understand through my body, my vulnerability, my oppressedness and how I oppress. Our simultaneity makes our difference felt rather than seen, and from this feeling I can think as a new action rather than as habitual recognition. This makes my understanding complicit, which I sense is part of the project of Muholi as a visual activist: to activate my position, so I might hear where I am looking from.

It is a generative and empowering way to see the interdependence of the visible and also of the invisible, of what is not here to make a wave, but nevertheless changes the pattern. And so I write about the photographs from a sonic sensibility, not to see sound, sonic artefacts, metaphors or allegories, all of which could easily be dismissed as fictional, esoteric and thus irrelevant. Instead, a sonic sensibility provides a rigorous practice of perception that eschews the distance of the image and enters into Muholi's confrontation to see plurality and responsibility. To sense the norm of my gaze, and the deceit of my position, and come to look another way.

Muholi's exhibition at the Gropius Bau in Berlin is arranged over nine rooms. With nine different titles, organizing different elements of their work, which together perform the complexity of sexuality and the complexity of race, and form what they term a visual activism: a practice of showing and narrating the consequence and responses to oppressive and violent political realities. The exhibition also includes self-portraits, manifesting Muholi's own participation, and bringing their own body into the vulnerability of being looked at while diffracting the gaze into the interdependent complexities of race, gender, sex, skin, class, history and a present Blackness that they feel 'is continuously performed by the privileged other'.

The images make, to take one of Muholi's own titles 'Only Half the Picture' (2002–2006). They do not show everything but make us participant and responsible for both the visible and the invisible: for what we think we see through our expectation and habits, and for what is told between pieces and between work and text, which together make visible a politics of violence and oppression against South Africa's LGBTQIA+ community. And so we become involved in the consequences of corrective rape of lesbian women in Soweto, carried out to enforce heterosexuality and gender conformity. Because the images do not invite a detached voyeurism. They do not show the spectacle of violence and they do not represent the other as victim, but confront und challenge a heteronormative gaze and expectation with self-care. They expand 'the narrative beyond victimhood and case numbers' by talking through marks on bodies, visible scars and invisible trauma, countered through gestures of intimacy and love.[6]

The marks on bodies are a witness to encounters and interactions that we cannot see but that determine the seen and our viewing. They tell a personal story and pluralize the body, away from the idea of representation into an invisible space of possibility, where bodies materialize through their stories, their truths and lived experience rather than according to pre-existing categories and expectations. The photographs make the body a witness to its own trauma and also empower the body in its own care and resistance. For if the body can speak of its pain, and be heard, it can resist and re-imagine through conversation and sharing. And if it can be a witness to its own repression and violence, it has to be taken seriously in (scientific) discourse and in law. It has to be allowed to represent itself in its diffractive complexity. To gain a voice not through correspondence, through a binary definition and pre-existing names, determined within the structure of law

---

[6]Zanele Muholi, quoted in exhibition wall text, Gropius Bau, Berlin, Germany, 26 November 2021 to 13 March 2022, https://www.berlinerfestspiele.de/en/berliner-fes tspiele/programm/bfs-gesamtprogramm/programmdetail_331291.html (accessed 13 March 2022).

and of science, but through its own plural and transforming materialization. To gain autonomy as a powerfully formless form that eschews grammar and definition, in favour of complex and contingent superimpositions of waves and skin.

Muholi's images of intimacy, closeness, caresses between lesbian couples articulate a form of resistance to an objectivity that thinks in binaries, that measures and names from a distance and according to a lexicon. They resist a hegemonic (scientific) view, that as universalizing principle colonizes knowledge and the body. Producing absolute truth and a consequent 'scientism' that is the understanding of science and knowledge as objective, rational, universal and empirical, not connected to cultural values, location, gender or racial specificity, which, however, and paradoxically, as a cultural value, legitimizes violence and exclusions of the very specificities it purports to be indifferent to.[7] Because the taxonomical thinking that underpins scientific objectivity and fact suffuses the social and establishes the norms that direct our gaze along colonial orientations that legitimize exclusions and oppressions through the deceit of their scientific neutrality.

The conventions and laws that seem crucial for scientific progress and that appear benign, and indeed the only possible way to work and think in the laboratory, reveal a darker politics in the social sphere. They reveal a politics of science which, according to Eric Voegelin, already since the sixteenth century excludes substance and experience in favour of mathematical measurement and data. An attitude which culminates, 'in the nine-teenth century, in the dictatorial prohibition, on the part of scientistic thinkers, against asking questions of a metaphysical nature'. Since within this scheme, as he subsequently suggests, 'All reality which is not accessible to sciences of phenomena is either irrelevant or, in the more radical form of the dogma.'[8] Science's rationale is built on exclusions. Its standards ensure repeatability and consensus, but they avoid the body

---

[7] Aikenhead, 'Whose Scientific Knowledge?', 151.

[8] Voegelin, 'Origins of Scientism', 462. Voegelin's text was written in 1948, shortly after the Second World War, in the United States, where he had moved to for his own political safety just before the war. It traces a clear connection between national socialism and scientism, and reads as a *plaidoyer* for a science that includes the body and experience in its practice, so it might not be a universal but a shared science of which we are a part in our contingency. This is not an anti-science statement. By contrast, it serves to chart a logical trajectory of how we get to anti-science, to the refusal of its discoveries, if we exclude the body and experience, and make a science that does not understand its relationality and contingency, that ignores its social responsibility and reality, but performs the violence of the universal and of mathematics.

in its lived contingency: in its sonic formlessness within which we meet, but which contradicts scientific measure. Such a scientific consciousness pervades society and politics. And within this socio-political consciousness of measures, distance, objectivity and universal truths, our lives and bodies can only be seen and judged in relation to pre-formed categories that make a line of correspondence. By contrast, a diffractive consciousness and creativity can see and hear more complex patterns of difference and non-linearity that do not need to judge but know by *being with*, in entangled difference. Thus, in the complex relationality of waves rather than lines, we recognize the violence of science, and how it treats the body, and how ultimately it legitimates social and political control. And we can come to decolonize our own gaze, to shift away from norms and see our own complicity through what we hear and sound.[9]

Barad understands diffraction as a feminist logic. She reminds us that feminist scholars have argued against reflexivity and distance on the ground that it ignores the complexities of gender, race, class, sexuality, ethnicity, religion and nationality. And she suggests that while science is concerned with the legitimacy of its own practices, it sees bodies as pre-formed social categories rather than 'gender-in-the-making' and in transformation.[10] Consequently, science has to diffract itself. It has to see its own *Beugung*, its own differences and patterns that come to view in the combination of bodies rather than their correspondence. This would not undermine scientific efficacy but enable the creative confrontation needed for social relevance. To make a 'better science' that is complimentary, adaptive, sustainable, as well as accessible and responsible to the people it is a science for.[11] To have a science within which the body is legitimate not despite but because of its contingency and transformation.

---

[9]Because, while decoloniality has a global aim, it is always necessarily a local endeavour – we can never decolonize someone else, but have to decolonize our own norms and expectations (Mignolo and Walsh, *On Decoloniality*, 2, 11). To this end, I propose sound making and listening, a sonic sensibility and practice, that do not follow the line but trouble its form, and thus that trouble ontologies of Western science, to create awareness of design and measurement biases, and to generate a shift in sensibility towards a plural science culture reflective of its position of privilege and dominance (Claudia Rankine, *Just Us. An American Conversation* (London: Penguin, 2020); Robin Angelo Di, *White Fragility* (Boston, MA: Beacon Press, 2018)).
[10]Karen Barad, *Meeting the Universe Halfway* (London: Duke University Press, 2007), 87.
[11]Laura Rival, 'Decolonising Knowledge and Pluralising Science', 2020, https://www.qeh.ox.ac.uk/content/decolonising-knowledge-and-pluralising-science/ (accessed August 2021).

Agreeing with Barad's identification of diffraction as feminist physical optics, I propose a feminist sonic physical optics that adds the relational and connecting logic of sound to the feminist effort against reflection and its parameters of distance, measurement, standards and norms. Thus I confront the violence of reflection and objectivity with the intimacy of sound and the relationality of its sensibility to reach an understanding of our simultaneity and the need for care. A physical optics as a sonic physical optics that senses and feels rather than sees the body, that generates bodies from diffraction patterns in contingent rhythms rather than as images of individuated forms, can speak individuality beyond correspondence to gender and names. It can speak the 'I' in its diffraction. Plural, overlapping 'I's, called the same and yet so very different, not as an absolute but as an interdependent difference that combines us all.

If diffraction, as Barad suggests, can think a feminist science, that is a science of entanglements, then we can also think an entangled arts and humanities, where we do not rely on reference and canonical history to give us distance and legitimacy, but where instead we listen to the body materializing its own story and truth. Here we come to know through performance and material practice rather than on the basis of theory and existing norms. And we can sense the norm and confront it with its 'post': to look at its contradictions and uncertainties and accept the bias of its measurement and the perfidy of its comforts. Consequently, we can perform knowledge from the body as a deliberate resistance to scientific distance and taxonomies, which as universal standards always necessarily exclude: excluding the body in its gestures and felt proximities, and take it as a pre-given category and form. And so we can include what is excluded in the image and in (theoretical) language through listening to skin as overlapping waves: to hear the body beyond speech from its physical marks and gestures. To see relationally, from sound, and come to appreciate human and more than human bodies through their entanglements rather than as individuated, politicized and socially pre-formed forms.

The bodies in the images of Muholi, and our bodies viewing with a sonic sensibility and care, perform the postnormal. Here the body is not a form of representation but a source of knowledge that is contingent, tacit, multisensorial. That materializes from what is seen and what remains invisible, and that is inclusive also of plural possibilities and even impossibilities: that which we cannot yet imagine or sense to be real, but that exists in the diffuse space of overlapping materialities. Such a body is produced in confrontation not through reflection. It does not offer an image or a measure for its legitimacy, but provides a complex encounter. In this way, while Muholi's project is specific to a particular community, its politics and place, it offers us a means to engage with other oppressed and marginal communities as communities of human and more than human bodies, whose knowledge lies not in their representation or measurement but in how we live together.

Exhalation: The practice of theory

By the time that theory, language and philosophy, have arrived at the postnormal, practice would already have been there. Theory lags. It always comes when the body has already moved. But what it can do, in its lateness and retrospection, is to open our thinking on practice, to legitimate it as the leading voice of theory and to declare theory itself a practice, subject to the same unreliability and ambiguities. It should do so in order to finally admit that theory is not more reliable, neutral or legitimate than practice. That it is not detached and apart from its object but generates it. And that its rigour lies not in words but on the body and its materialization with other human and more than human bodies, in their interdependencies and in-betweens, from where it can be plural and speak in different registers.

Theory does not and cannot perform a critique *of*. It too generates materializations *with*: from words as things and a body in practice. However, inner disciplinary referentiality and a formidable trust in language and linear history, as guarantors of intelligibility, constrict the contingency of these materializations and confer on theory a sense of reliability. This is a reliability, however, that was gained by doing violence to the body of the work, and the body of human and more than human things, by framing their diffuse contingency rather than allowing it to take shape, and by excluding what does not fit within its scheme. Theory in order to claim a universal and hegemonic articulation, distances itself from the vagaries of practice and a plural body, which it describes within its terms but does not allow to speak its own. Instead, it sets up norms and expectations, constructing disciplinary lines and borders, that ensure readability and consensus, demonstrated by the ability to reference and evidence its findings away from the thing and the body theorized. Thus, it produces a reflective theory of correspondence, and stays in comparison and reassurance with its own articulation, rather than undoing and transforming its materiality and language to find overlaps and simultaneities with anything and anybody at all. In this way, theory aims to convey scientific value, and shares science's exclusionary rationale, when in reality, theory, at the moment of its practice, writes from a plural body and with love.

References and citations are protagonists in a performance of affection and preference. The closeness of theorists to those that they invite into their texts is decisive and telling. Its intimacy is written in phrases such as, 'as a Heideggerian…', 'thinking here with Deleuze…', 'Working from Derrida…'. They admit affection and even a love that surely must impede detachment and measured criticality, which is deferred to the names mentioned. This affection makes theory a practice of love and admiration, but also, in its own terms, renders it untrustworthy, non-objective, lacking in distance and criticality. It is the paradox of great affection towards those we quote in order to remain objective that closes the distance that through its claim to objectivity grants the argument legitimacy. And so in truth, theory does not write arguments but critical fictions, and generates an actual possible world that only retains its borders and pre-formed form through exclusions and through patriarchy; through conventions, paternal lines and a fear of becoming unrecognizable, dismissable. Because this affection is not open to everybody. These are particular entanglements, unspokenly selective and hyper-normative without asking after the criteria that make a source more worthy and able to carry our arguments. Thus, they remain paternal loves and network biases.

What theorists are we allowed to fall in love with? What reference evidences the marks on our body?

We need to question our likes and loves, who we trust and take in evidence, and who we do not permit into discourse. To come to understand them not as neutral, historically assured standard-bearers of quality, but as the result of patriarchal scholarship, our own orientation and its inevitable limitations that constrain who we can think with and how. The fiction of reference and citation, just like measurements and taxonomies, speak of love and prejudice: of the order through which we see the world.

In response, we need to listen to expand the field of reference into inexhaustibility, so it ceases to be a field, a boundaried territory of theory and philosophy, and becomes a volume of indivisible interdependencies where the impossible becomes possible and quality is a matter of practice, perpetually.

Because, and paradoxically, the deep entanglements between canonical theorists and how we write with them prevent the critical distance sought in their reference, as there is no gap into which a neutral voice can slip to give us analysis and interpretation. Such gaps are an illusion. A mirage of language that gives us differentiated pronouns and prepositions that present a spatial and temporal separation, when in thinking as practice we are always already entangled. There is no outside.

In an essay written before the pandemic, I discuss such an outside in relation to Erin Manning and Brian Massumi's book *Thought in the Act* (2014).[12] In the introduction, they present the outside of philosophy as a 'generative environment' that offers itself to think collaboratively the act of doing the impossible,[13] whereby the impossible is not really what does not or cannot exist, but what we do not yet know, giving collaboration a generative and future capacity rather than an interpretative role. Their close focus on work, on movements and expressions of the body and speech rather than language, attaches a positive and curious energy to the excessive, to that which goes beyond and stands outside. Accordingly, language articulates not as a precarious bridge nor as an inevitable gap but as a deliberate breach 'in the fragile difference between models of thought in the act', breaching the limits of language to speak its excess, to speak outside the disciplinary boundary and expectation.[14] To identify this excess, Manning and Massumi recall the break with meaning in teenage speech: 'It's like this. Just like, sad.' This phrase does not pursue designation and definition but voices a more refracted sense on the border of speechlessness, uttering sensation. 'It marks an affective overflow in speech.' It is just like sad is: it 'overfills, its designation', and opens towards the possibility of a sensorial sense articulating the impossible.[15]

Re-reading their text now, it becomes clear that the notion of excess and the outside is a compromise I am not willing to engage anymore. Identifying the affective and refracted inarticulation of teenage utterance as excess of proper speech is an appeasement of language and disciplinary boundaries, which guards speech's line and ducks out of confrontation. The excess and outside at once enable a different thinking, positioning the impossible, but they also legitimize disciplinary norms, shoring up boundaries and lack of permeability. By contrast, I am interested in the excess inside, which remains invisible but holds the potential for a different visibility. Therefore, I am interested in sound, in listening and the making and studying of sound, as

[12]Salomé Voegelin, 'Writing Sonic Fictions: Literature as a Portal into the Possibility of Art Research', in *Artistic Research and Literature*, ed. Corinna Caduff and Tan Wälchli (Germany: Wilhelm Fink, 2019), 99–109, open access https://www.fink.de/view/book/edcoll/9783846763339/BP000011.xml. (accessed 10 July 2022).
[13]Erin Manning, and Brian Massumi, *Thought in the Act: Passages in the Ecology of Experience* (Minneapolis: University of Minnesota Press, 2014), vii.
[14]Ibid.
[15]Ibid., 34.

an interloper and troubling force. As a transversal materiality and practice that does not need its own discipline, and does not want to sit outside, but that permeates and infects every discipline with its invisible and dark side, which is the depth of our interdependencies. From this depth, we sense rather than know marks on bodies through their overlaps with our own, and are enabled to see ourselves looking, to catch a normative gaze in the postness of now, which holds the potential of a different future, generated from diffuse combinations rather than straight and parallel lines.

In this sense, the postnormal embraces the love of the theorist, but also shows them its root and bias, and calls on them to love more audaciously, more variedly and from further afield also what they do not know and whose language and body they do not recognize. Thus, it confronts theory with the source and culture of normativity and challenges us to disinvest from the lines made by disciplines, canons, history, reflection and their search for correspondences. To practice disaffiliation:[16] to trouble philosophical traditions where they are unable to grasp what practice does in its plural and material expressions. And to instead foster a theoretical sensibility that does not evidence and reference but is in conversation with plural bodies and things, generative of a theory that brings embodied, tacit, feminist, indigenous, local and plural knowledges to the fore.

The pandemic has re-framed the body beyond theory, in a network of bodies combined in breath, in air, in overlapping and porous waves. This sense of an interdependent and codependent world and simultaneous bodies gained cannot be ignored in our haste to get back to normalcy. Instead, we have to move to a postnormal that practices an 'arts and humanities of entanglements' with a science of entanglements, where theory is a practice of a body *with*: with human and more than human bodies, performing their transformative overlaps and simultaneity.

Such a postnormal entanglement has a sonic sensibility. It is just like sound, porous and indivisible. Thus, it is a sonic thinking, a thinking through the invisible and relational logic of sound, which can make its possibilities accessible and its practice feasible. There is no outside of

---

[16]Manthia Diawara describing the philosophy of Édouard Glissant, writes about his rebellious thesis of disaffiliation as 'breaking with a geneology and tradition of Western and non-western philosophies concerned with binary opposition and contradiction' and moving 'beyond oppositional discourse of the same and the other, operating instead with a new vision of difference as an assembler of the "dissimilars"'. 'Édouard Glissant's Worldmentality: An Introduction to *One World in Relation*', https://www.documenta14. de/en/south/34_edouard_glissant_s_worldmentality_an_introduction_to_one_world_ in_relation (accessed 13 February 2022).

sound, there is no excess. Everything is sounding, and I am always within and participating even in what appears silent and inaudible. Making my own sounds while listening. Sound as concept and materiality does not present the discontinuity of disciplinary lines. Instead, it presents a continuity, not as perpetually the same, but as a 'Fortgesetzter Versuch', as a continuous attempt, whose difference is boundless. Therefore, sound does not invite additions to the line. It does not simply add names to canonical thinking, but implodes the line through overlaps and diffuse simultaneities, offering an entangled view that confronts the norms of individuation, of a boundaried self and a boundaried discourse, from the postness of our interdependencies.

This entangled view of postnormality does not produce the reality of objectivity. It does not enable distance and interpretation. Instead, it generates materializations and critical proximities that force responsibility to bodies and gestures as well as to silences not heard. This is not the responsibility to a pre-formed order, but to the disorder of an unbounded field in excess of itself, everywhere. Thus, it cannot be reached through translation and from how we see it represented, as measurements and through language, or what lies outside. Instead, it demands the competency to know the world from how we generate it together, in a sonic physical optics, sensing the relational complexities of asymmetries and contingencies.

To develop this competency and come to 'see' in entanglements, I propose to establish sound studies as a transversal study: as a study and methodology that traverses disciplinary lines to get to know the world from its diffuse contingencies, unstable relationalities and potent interdependencies. Such a transversal sound studies does not define an autonomous discipline but interlopes in every field to develop a 'sonic competency' that thinks relationality and equips us to diffuse hegemonic knowledge strands and to handle the 'wicked problems' that describe the interdependencies of a viral world.[17] The 'wicked' describes the

---

[17]Horst Rittel and Melvin Webber use, or rather reuse, the term 'wicked problems' in the 1970s to describe social planning and governance problems which are inherently complex, entangled, have too many contradictory elements and do not propose a clear path to their solution (HorstRittel and Melvin Webber, 'Dilemmas in a General Theory of Planning', *Policy Sciences* 4, no. 2 (1973): 155–69). This notion of 'wickedness' more presently offers an important conceptualization of the intertwined issues of climate change, migration and public health such as the pandemic, and so on. Such problems and their entanglement are called wicked 'because of the incomplete knowledge of effects and interdependencies, because it involves actors operating in different sectors and at different levels, because all possible actions have uncertain effects and because they are intertwined with other problems in complex and, to a large extent, unmanageable

unpredictable and incomplete knowledge effects and interdependencies of a contemporary world, when climate, public health, scarcity of resources and migration present themselves as intertwined and unmanageable, and the world as codependent. In response, sonic competencies offer a new paradigm for the humanities and the sciences, who in their desire for reference and evidence, objectivity and measurement, have constrained themselves to too narrow lines to deal with their entanglements.

Therefore, I argue that it is sound studies with its radical non-disciplinarity and interloping potential that has the capacity to access the world in its complex relationality. To produce a generative knowledge not from outside but through embedded listening, creating hybrid (un)disciplinarities: listening in and with every discipline, to unperform its borders and the violence of singular hegemonic knowledge paths; hearing entanglements and complex contradictions, uncertainties and idiosyncrasies, to contribute new solutions from sound's own wickedness.

Thus, rather than continuing along disciplinary lines that are exclusive and detrimental to understanding and responding to an interdependent world and bodies in combination, sound studies as a transversal studies dissolves disciplinary boundaries as well as the violence and exclusions that they perform, through a diffuse contingency and a sonic competency that remains incompetent in relation to objectivity as distance, but is competent in relation to a practice that is accountable to human and more than human bodies. In this way, we empower the body from its marks and gestures. Producing a counter-theory, a counter-archive, a counter-epistemology that knows from practice and with bodies appearing through their interdependence rather than represented from measurements and the bias of its science.

Muholi's photographs are an inspiration to this thinking. Their affective and participative counter-archive of the LGBTQIA+ community in South Africa enables a counter to the norm that is not antinomic but stands in continuous confrontation, working with the norm to show its gaze and pluralize its vision.

Postnormal, transversal sound studies are decidedly not the construction of a solid discipline. They are not the pursuit of a conventional framework of theory and scholarship, teaching and learning, and neither are they its outside and excess. Instead, they are an attempt to find and foster a sonic sensibility and relational logic in everything. To collaborate, not to bridge disciplinary boundaries, but to agitate, to unsettle and trouble them: to confront each field with its invisible and indivisible dimension that is inside.

---

systems' (Per Morton Shiefloe, 'The Corona Crisis: A Wicked Problem', *Scandinavian Journal of Public Health* 49 (2021): 5–8, 5).

In this way, every study, every discipline and field of research and work, can profit from the practice of sound, as sonic sensibility, as a means to hear, as in think, in overlaps and interdependencies, rather than attempt the separation of what comes to consequence and sense together. The transversal studying from sound, through a sonic physical optics, helps to question disciplinary frames of reference and their constitutive norms. It serves to add to their methodologies new approaches and methods that can deal with the complex interdependencies and overlapping bodies of a postnormal world: to challenge a theoretical norm from a relational 'post' of now.

I promote the founding of transversal sound studies, that is the practice of a theory that listens to everything and across every field of work and research, as a radical demand, because I know the resistance of norms, cross-hatched from disciplinary privilege, comfort, bias and professional investment will be so great, and institutional habits and boundaries so entrenched, that it will not happen. And so I can demand it even more flamboyantly, outrageously, determinedly, because I feel it is a good way to think at least its actual possibility: the promise of a necessary competency to live in a connected world, and a vital ability to change the scientific consciousness of binaries, taxonomies, certainties and lines that ignores the proximities of its own infatuations with those it references in evidence of its objective truths. I also articulate sound studies not as an essentialized undertaking but as a portal into a 'multisensory studies', that does not stop at invisibility but senses it as a cause, as Wolf did, to hear, smell, taste, see and so on differently, and to create a physical image of the world in its entanglements.[18]

On this point, writing about *Weltbilder*, Images of the World, Wolf suggests that

Ihnen (den Physikern) mag es leichter fallen als den Schreibern, zu definieren, woran sie arbeiten – sie wollen herausfinden, aus welchem Material die Welt besteht; aber merkwürdigerweise brauchen sie – je kleiner die Teilchen werden, mit denen sie es zu tun haben, je schwieriger exakte Messungen – eingestandenermaßen eine unmessbare Größe: die schöpferische Phantasie. Wer weiß, ob nicht in ihren geheimsten Stunden der blasphemische Gedanke sie anwandelt, dass eigentlich sie es sind, die die Welt erfinden.[19]

---

[18]Wolf, '*Fortgesetzter Versuch*', 7.
[19] 'They (the physicists) may find it easier than the writers to define what they are working on – they want to enquire what the world is made of; but paradoxically, the smaller the particles they deal with, the more difficult exact measurements become – the

From this idea, that we do not measure but generate the world through our measures of creative imagination, and the responsibility that follows this insight, I reaffirm, here at the end of this book that 'post-pandemic' we cannot go to a new normal that builds on the normal that went before, on its linear sense of correspondence and on its patriarchal line and knowledge networks. Instead, we have to embrace a postnormal that is a forever 'unnormal', where the sense of normality itself might be opened to different and plural ideas of how things are generated, imagined and known through their postness, that is the tardiness of theory and the confrontation of its self-evident measure by practice, creating an invisible image of the world in entanglements of diffuse and overlapping bodies and an interdependent world.[20]

---

more they require an unquantifiable measure: the creative imagination. Who knows whether in their most secret hours they are not infected by the blasphemous thought that it is actually them who invent the world? (Wolf, 'Fortgesetzter Versuch', 28)

[20]Christa Wolf, the East German author, who silently accompanied this chapter from the opening citation, has a difficult position in literary and political history. She is placed at once too close to the regime of the GDR (German Democratic Republic), enjoying its favours and preference, and distrusted by it. She apparently spied for the Stasi in the 1950s, and later was spied upon by them, and in my simultaneous timespace universe of sound, she is today a double agent.

I loved her writing as a teenager, particularly her book *Kassandra* from 1983, a story about the Trojan War, blind seers and the question of how we can know when the pre-war starts. Reading her again now reminds me of the capacity of time to defy its own chronology, and to be at once now and then, here and there. It instils in me the desire to practice such a simultaneous time and its equivalent: a concurrent space to generate the plural simultaneity of the world in which the uncertainty of time generates an elastics of intervals and a permeability of boundaries, which shows in dark explosions of everything at once and lets us think relationally; to reach with you a world that is not chronological, and spatial, but a radical simultaneity of thought and the cacophony of voices from here and there, the past and the present audible all at once. Listening as an expanded practice appears to offer one such time and place shifting device. Through listening and a sonic sensibility, I can access where the world loses its surface orientation and maps, as well as its time signature and chronology and implodes into an entanglement, where things know themselves through their simultaneity with everything else.

Wolf writes her ideas on the *Fortgesetzter Versuch*, the continued and radical approach towards a new world of prose, from a hope in socialism:

Das heißt, die Prosa kann sich nur mit gedanklichen Strömungen und gesellschaftlichen Bewegungen verbinden, die der Menschheit eine Zukunft geben, die frei sind von den jahrhundertealten und den brandneuen Zauberformeln der Manipulierung und selbst das Experiment nicht scheuen. Das heißt, ich sehe eine tiefe Übereinstimmung zwischen dieser Art zu schreiben mit der sozialistischen Gesellschaft. Bewiesen

Zu schreiben kann erst beginnen, wem die Realität nicht mehr selbstverständlich ist.[21]

---

ist, daß Ausbeutergesellschaften nicht fähig sind, der Menschheit eine Zukunft zu sichern, die diesen Namen verdient.

('Prose can only connect to philosophical trends and social movements which give humanity a future, which are free from the century old as well as the brand new magic formulas of manipulation and which do not shy away from experimentation. In other words, I see a deep coincidence between such a way of writing and socialist society. As it is evident that exploitative social models are incapable to provide a future for humanity which would deserve its name'. Wolf, '*Fortgesetzter Versuch*', 30).

At this juncture, where the exploitations of neo-liberalism and of communist socialism have stepped into a timespace simultaneity and global interdependence, we can be inspired by her call against precarity, and for a generative literature and science whatever political spectrum we are on. However, I lack her hope and trust in governmental politics to provide a different frame. Instead, I take Zanele Muholi's visual activism and add a sonic activism, to practice with Karen Barad and Donna Haraway a sonic physical optics, as expanded listening, to see an entangled world, and reach a transversal consciousness, that includes plural gestures and marks on human and more than human bodies to generate how we live together, postnormally.

[21]'Only those can begin to write for whom reality has ceased to be self-evident' (Wolf, '*Fortgesetzter Versuch*', 31).

Performing walls IX

Stand half a meter away from a wall
facing it.
Let yourself fall into the wall
while screaming
don't catch yourself.

BIBLIOGRAPHY

Acker, Kathy. 'Against Ordinary Language: The Language of the Body'. In *The Last Sex: Feminism and Outlaw Bodies*, edited by Arthur Kroker and Marilouise Kroker, 22–7. Basingstoke, UK: Macmillan, 1993.

Ahmed, Sara. 'Orientation Matters'. In *New Materialism, Ontology, Agency, and Politics*, edited by Diana Coole and Samantha Frost, 234–57. London: Duke University Press, 2010.

Ahmed, Sara. 'Orientation: Towards a Queer Phenomenology'. *GLQ: A Journal of Lesbian and Gay Studies* 12, no. 4 (2006): 543–74.

Aikenhead, Glen. 'Whose Scientific Knowledge? The Colonizer and the Colonized'. In *Science Education as/for Sociopolitical Action*, edited by W. M. Roth and J. Desautels, 151–66. New York: Peter Lang International, Academic Publishers, 2002.

Aikenhead, Glen. 'Border Crossing into the Subculture of Science'. *Studies in Science Education* 27 (1996): 1–52.

Al-Samman, Ghada. 'The Lover of Blue Writing above the Sea!' In *The Poetry of Arab Women, A Contemporary Anthology*, translated by Saad Ahmed and Miriam Cooke, edited by Nathalie Handal, 274–6. Northampton, MA: Interlink Books, 2015.

Angelo Di, Robin. *White Fragility*. Boston, MA: Beacon Press, 2018.

Balibar, Étienne. *Equaliberty*. London: Duke University Press, 2014.

Balibar, Étienne. *Violence and Civility, On the Limits of Political Philosophy*, translated by G. M. Goshgarian. New York: Columbia University Press, 2015.

Barad, Karen. *Meeting the Universe Halfway*. London: Duke University Press, 2007.

Barad, Karen. 'Posthumanist Performativity: Towards an Understanding of How Matter Comes to Matter'. *Signs: Journal of Women in Culture and Society* 28, no. 3, *Gender and Science: New Issues* (Spring 2003): 801–31.

Barz, Gregory, and William Cheng. *Queering the Field, Sounding Out Ethnomusicology*. UK: Oxford University Press, 2019.

Braidotti, Rosi. *Nomadic Subjects, Embodiment and Sexual Difference in Contemporary Feminist Theory*, 2nd edn. New York: Columbia University Press, 2011.

Butler, Judith. *Bodies That Matter: On the Discursive Limits of Sex*. New York: Routledge, 1993.

Cixous, Hélène, and Catherine Clément. *The Newly Born Woman*. London: I. B. Tauris, 1996.

Daston, Lorraine, and Peter Galison. *Objectivity*. Brooklyn: Zone Books, 2007.

Diawara, Manthia. 'Édouard Glissant's Worldmentality: An Introduction to *One World in Relation*'. https://www.documenta14.de/en/south/34_edouard_glissant_s_worldmentality_an_introduction_to_one_world_in_r elation (accessed 13 February 2022).

Dolphijn, Rick, and Iris van der Tuin. *New Materialism: Interviews & Cartographies*, 48–70. Ann Arbor, MI: Open Humanities Press, 2012.

Džuverović, Lina, and Irene Revell. 'Lots of Shiny Junk at the Art Dump: The Sick and Unwilling Curator'. *Parse* 9 (Spring 2019). http://parsejournal.com/article/lots-of-shiny-junk-at-the-art-dump-the-sick-and-unwilling-curator/ (accessed 17 November 2020).

Feld, Steven. 'Acoustemology'. In *Keywords in Sound*, edited by David Novak and Matt Sakakeeny, 12–21. London: Duke University Press, 2015.

Fanon, Franz. *The Wretched of the Earth*, translated by Constance Farrington. New York: Grove Press, 1961.

Foucault, Michel. *Power/Knowledge, Selected Interviews and Other Writing*, edited by Colin Gordon. New York: Phanteon Books, 1980.

Foucault, Michel. *The Archeology of Knowledge*, translated by A. M. Sheridan Smith. New York: Phanteon Books, 1972.

Galván-Alvarez, Enrique. 'Epistemic Violence and Retaliation: The Issue of Knowledges in "Mother India"'. *Atlantis* 32, no. 2 (December 2010): 11–26.

Grosz, Elizabeth. *Volatile Bodies: Towards a Corporeal Feminism*. Bloomington: Indiana University Press, 1994.

Groys, Boris. 'The Politics of Installation'. *e-flux, Journal* 2 (January 2009). https://www.e-flux.com/journal/02/68504/politics-of-installation/ (accessed 17 November 2020).

Haraway, Donna. *Staying with the Trouble*: *Making Kin in the Chthulucene*. Durham, NC: Duke University Press, 2016.

Jones, Alison, and Kuni Jenkins. 'Indigenous Discourse and "the Material" A Post-Interpretivist Argument'. *International Review of Qualitative Research* 1, no. 2 (August 2008): 125–44.

Krauss, Rosalind. 'Sculpture in the Expanded Field'. *October* 8 (Spring 1979): 30–44.

Kristeva, Julia. *Revolution in Poetic Language*. New York: Columbia University Press, 1984.

LaBelle, Brandon. 'Restless Acoustics, Emergent Publics'. In *The Routledge Companion to Sounding Art*, edited by Marcel Cobussen, Vincent Meelberg and Barry Truax, 275–85. New York: Routledge, 2017.

Le Guin, Ursula K. *The Unreal and the Real Volume 2: Selected Stories: Outer Space, Inner Lands*. London: Orion, 2015.

Lorde, Audre. 'The Master's Tools Will Never Dismantle the Master's House'. In *Your Silence Will Not Protect You*, 89–93. UK: Silver Press, 2017.

Manning, Erin, and Brian Massumi. *Thought in the Act: Passages in the Ecology of Experience*. Minneapolis: University of Minnesota Press, 2014.

McClary, Susan, and Sam de Boise. 'An Interview with Professor Susan McClary: The Development of Research on Gender and Music'. *Per Musi: Scholarly Music Journal* 39 (2019): 1–9, e19390.

Merleau-Ponty, Maurice. *The Visible and the Invisible*, translated by Alphonso Lingis, edited by Claude Lefort. Evanston, IL: Northwestern University Press, 1968.

Mignolo, Walter D., and CatherineWalsh. *On Decoloniality, Concepts, Analytics and Praxis*. London: Duke University Press, 2018.

Muholi, Zanele. Exhibition Wall Text, Gropius Bau, Berlin, Germany, 26 November 2021 to 13 March 2022. https://www.berlinerfestspiele.de/en/berliner-festspiele/programm/bfs-gesamtprogramm/programmdetail_331291.html (accessed 13 February 2022).

Ndikung, Bonaventure Soh Bejeng. *The Delusions of Care*. Berlin: Archive Books, 2021.

Ndikung, Bonaventure Soh Bejeng. 'Where Do We Go from Here: For They Shall Be Heard'. *Frieze*, 28 October 2018. https://www.frieze.com/article/where-do-we-go-here-they-shall-be-heard (accessed August 2021).

Piper, Adrian. 'Notes on Funk I-II//1985/83'. In *Participation Documents of Contemporary Art*, 130–4, edited by Claire Bishop. Massachusetts: MIT Press, 2006.

Prescod-Weinstein, Chanda. *The Disordered Cosmos: A Journey into Dark Matter, Spacetime, and Dreams Deferred*. US: Bold Type Books, 2021.

Rankine, Claudia. *Just Us. An American Conversation*. London: Penguin, 2020.

Rebentisch, Juliane. *Ästhetik der Installation*. Germany: Edition Suhrkamp, 2003.

Rittel, Horst, and Melvin Webber. 'Dilemmas in a General Theory of Planning'. *Policy Sciences* 4, no. 2 (1973): 155–69.

Rival, Laura. 'Decolonising Knowledge and Pluralising Science'. 2020. https://www.qeh.ox.ac.uk/content/decolonising-knowledge-and-pluralising-science/ (accessed August 2021).

Rocha Sepulveda, Aleyda. 'Territorialising from Within: protocolos [en tránsito] para atender lo de adentro'. *Border-Listening/Escucha-Liminal* 1 (2020): 93–105.

Russell, Legacy. *Glitch Feminism, a Manifesto*. London: Verso, 2020.

Shiefloe, Per Morton. 'The Corona Crisis: A Wicked Problem'. *Scandinavian Journal of Public Health* 49 (2021): 5–8.

Shildrick, Margrit. *Leaky Bodies and Boundaries: Feminism, Postmodernism and (Bio) Ethics*. London: Routledge, 1997.

Shildrick, Margrit, and Janet Price. *Vital Signs, Feminists Reconfigurations of the Bio/logical Body*. Edinburgh, UK: Edinburgh University Press, 1998.

Somerville, Shioban B. *Queering the Color Line, Race and Invention of Homosexuality in American Culture*. US: Duke University Press, 2020.

Stoever, Jennifer Lynn. *The Sonic Color Line, Race and the Cultural Politics of Listening*, New York: New York University Press, 2016.

Voegelin, Eric. 'The Origins of Scientism'. *Social Research* 15, no. 4 (December 1948): 462–94.

Voegelin, Salomé. *Listening to Noise and Silence: Hearing the Continuum of Sound*. New York: Bloomsbury, 2010.

Voegelin, Salomé. 'Singing Philosophy: Deviating Voices and Rhythms without a Time Signature'. *Open Philosophy* 4 (2021): 284–91.

Voegelin, Salomé. *The Political Possibility of Sound*. New York: Bloomsbury, 2018.

Voegelin, Salomé. 'Writing Sonic Fictions: Literature as a Portal into the Possibility of Art Research'. In *Artistic Research and Literature*, edited by Corinna Caduff and Tan Wälchli, 99–109. Germany: Wilhelm Fink, 2019. https://www.fink.de/view/book/edcoll/9783846763339/BP000011.xml. (accessed July 2022).

Walker, Kara. Documentary Video. https://www.youtube.com/watch?v=tV_L 3fceGNA (accessed 27 December 2021).

Wolf, Christa. *Fortgesetzter Versuch: Aufsätze Gespräche Essays*. Leipzig: Reclam, 1982.

LIST OF WORKS

Boer de, Manon. *Think about Wood, Think about Metal*. Documentary film, 48 minutes, Colour, Stereo, 4:3, 16 mm Film, Belgium, 2011.

Cage, John. *4′ 33″*, performance premiered by David Tudor, 29 August 1952, Woodstock, New York.

Cardiff, Janet, and George Bures Miller. *The Dark Pool*, Installation at Oxford Museum of Modern Art, UK, 2009, orig. 1995.

Carr, Kate. *Hawkes End – River Sowe Junction – A Sonic Transect of the Sometimes Absent River Sherbourne*, Sound Work Produced for the 2021 Coventry Biennale in the UK.

Fullman, Ellen. *In the Sea*, Super Viaduct, SV 174, 2020, orig. 1987.

Humeau, Marguerite, and Lafawndah. *WEEDS*, Swiss Church in London, 2021.

Muholi, Zanele, at the Gropius Bau, Berlin, Germany, 26 November 2021 to 13 March 2022.

Morris, Robert. *Work Untitled (Mirrored Cubes)*, Installation at Green Gallery, New York, 1965.

Piper, Adrian, *Funk Lessons*, an audience-interactive performance staged at various locations, between 1982 and 1984.

Walker, Kara. *Fons Americanus*, Sculpture, from Cork, Soft Wood and Metal, Coated in Resin. Tate Modern Hyundai Commission, 2019.

INDEX